DUAL MISSION

A true story about a Secret Service Agent and his investigative experiences to include his battle with the New York Mafia!

NINO PERROTTA

I dedicate this book to the men and women of the United States Secret Service who manage successfully the daily challenges the job brings to each of you and your loved ones. I want to also share the dedication with my son Antonio and daughter Valentina. I hope that you both learn a few "interesting" things about dad while reading this book and the challenges life can present when you push yourself and others towards a higher cause.

Table of Contents

Introduction

I was born on July 29, 1967, at Mount Vernon Hospital, the first child to a young mother and father from Paolisi, Italy. Antonio Perrotta and Luigina Falco were married in Paolisi, which is a commune in the province of Benevento in the Italian region of Campania. A small town located about 35 km northeast of Naples and about 20 km southwest of Benevento. A place with a population of no more than 1,900 people. Today, you can find many Falco and Perrotta families listed in the Italian telephone directory. From the period of 1876 and 1976, during the mass emigration from Italy, the United States was the largest single recipient of Italian immigrants in the world.

In 1850, less than 4,000 Italians were reportedly in the U.S. However, in 1880, merely 4 years after the influx of Italian immigrants migrated, the population skyrocketed to 44,000, and by 1900, it reached a high of 484,027. From 1880 to 1900, southern Italian immigrants became the predominant Italian immigrant group in the United States. It remained this way throughout the mass migration. Despite the increased numbers, the Italians were not the largest foreign-origin group in American cities. They were outnumbered by groups migrating for decades before them. At their peak, Italians made up a mere 1.5 percent of the United States population.

The impact on and experience of the Italian immigrant in America was not as great as that of their counterparts in other countries like

Argentina and Brazil. This was due to the fact that hundreds of thousands of immigrants from nations all over the world were migrating to the United States at the same time. In addition, American-born natives had already made up the majority ethnic group. The Italians did play a major role, though, socially with individuals rising to national stature in many different fields.

My father and mother came to New York with virtually nothing. They had no money, no job, and very little prospects. What they did have in abundance was, in fact, priceless—they had intense hope and an unyielding dream. An aspiration shared and passed along by our aunts and uncles who had arrived on American soil years prior. After their wedding, my mother and father gathered what few items they received as gifts. Since my mother was an only child, her mom, my grandmother Luisa Gallo Falco, was part of the wedding offerings the newlyweds received.

My grandfather had committed suicide when his wife Luisa was only a few weeks pregnant. I know very little of him and what was shared made little to no sense. He was allegedly at a market and accused of theft. In the period of time they apprehended the real thief, he had slit his throat while in prison. He was able to speak to his bride and state the embarrassment as too great to bear and was found dead shortly thereafter. My grandmother, who raised my mother as a single parent, did everything she could for her daughter. As a young girl, she sent her daughter to school in Naples to learn the art of being a seamstress. This was not an easy task, and it showed that my grandmother was determined to give my mom everything possible at that time.

I have spent my entire adult life serving our nation in some type of security or law enforcement capacity, from my time as a college student in the U.S. ARMY R.O.T.C. program, eventually commissioned as a 2nd lieutenant trained in military intelligence, leading men and woman my same age, to a rookie detective investigator assigned as a special investigator for the New York State Organized Crime Task Force (OCTF), to my eventual commission as a special agent in the United States Secret Service.

My experiences are as varied as the mission of each organization, the locations in which I have worked, and the very people with whom I have shared an incredible journey. A road which, at times, felt too long, and the trip, at times, too desolate; nonetheless, one which has been a privilege beyond my ability to describe to have been a part of.

I have held a government security clearance since 1989. However, in the summer of 2017, I intend to embark on a new journey. I will no longer carry a gun and a badge as my retirement awaits. Time, regrettably, has passed where my official service to the country will conclude, while I take on a new, yet to be determined, role. Although a major accomplishment in my better than two decades of service was my investigation of the mob, in reality, the better part of my federal law enforcement career had nothing to do with investigating organized crime figures. Nonetheless, the time I spent taking on a high – profile financial crimes investigation had its internal challenges. The Secret Service is a dual mission agency, charged with protection of the President and Foreign Dignitaries as well as investigations to safeguard our nation's financial infrastructure. The mission which receives most priority however is its mission of protection. Unfortunately in my experience, its investigative mission was secondary. Therefore since I was determined to handle the case as a priority, the "Dual Mission" conflict between my duties, both with protection and investigations, where always in the forefront.

The thought that my time as a federal agent will soon be over, and a new career will replace it fills me with a sense of grief and optimism. I know I will soon mourn the passing of what has been an all-consuming and fulfilling job…no a life style. The thought of not performing my duty to serve the public as an agent is almost unfathomable. However, as I age and watch my two beautiful children grow, I realize there is so much more ahead of me. A new course awaits in which, together, with my wife who I met in Washington D.C. upon my return from Bulgaria we will pen the direction and content of our life chapters.

This book is my effort to share some of my uncommon experiences over the course of a lifetime spent growing up in an Italian immigrant family and coming to age and professional maturity in the realm of a law enforcement career. I truly hope the reader will find some enjoyment and value in my accounts and, at times, unique perspective of things. I am also motivated by the potential that one day when I am long gone, my son and daughter may, one day, as adults, read these pages and get to know their dad in a way that had previously alluded them.

The pages in this book will attempt to capture my energy, personal drive, and commitment spent on achieving my goal of becoming a special agent, a coveted title and topic of countless books, movies, and TV shows. My days as a young boy were spent daydreaming about being a "good guy" fighting the Mafia and making my dreams of being a federal agent an eventual reality. Like people of all professions, I experienced struggles, both, on and off the job. My particular skirmishes climbing the law enforcement career ladder and maneuvering in and around the spheres of justice were, at times, monumental, unexpected, and occasionally, entertaining.

As I have matured, I realize that for most of my life, I was completely misunderstood by most, including my family and friends. Throughout my early career, it often appeared that my fellow agents and supervisors did not quite get me, my motivations and authenticity often maligned and misunderstood. I have come to accept that I contributed to this misconception and false labeling in large part because of my high level of energy.

As a young man in my 20s, I was always on. I was filled with tremendous vigor that overflowed, at times in the wrong time, wrong place, and definitely, to a wrong audience. One thing for certain though and cannot be disputed is that I was, and remain, loyal. My loyalty to friends and mission was never questioned. Looking back, one thing remained constant despite my energy levels having tapered off a bit. I always got results. I always found the bad guy. I always made consequential investigations and arrests.

My desire for success and willingness to put forth the extra effort into making my dreams a reality, combined with my excessive liveliness, ultimately led to my commission into a revered, proud, and storied law enforcement agency in the country: the United States Secret Service. What I did with my newfound authority and the often-unorthodox methods employed to achieve my childhood dreams are shared in the following pages.

A consistent theme throughout my 25-year career in this profession is the extreme dedication and patriotism of those with whom I served. I have worked alongside the very best people in law enforcement, bar none. My intention in this book, however, ambitious, is to provide an accurate account of my unique law enforcement experiences. I say they are unique in that they were quite often found in the daily, and often, mundane, routine of just living my life. There are countless opportunities for success and fulfillment when one is open to the nuances that exist in simply being present to your surroundings. My journey begins by going back to, as my father used to say, "the old country"—Italy, the birthplace of my mother and father.

1

The Fugitive and Me

At times upon moments of reflection, I look back at my life during a unique decade as a law enforcement agent with mixed emotions, but mostly with great pride and respect. These memories bring me to a distant country where, only as a child, did I imagine myself working in such a dangerous place. It was around 6:00 p.m., on a Saturday evening in Sophia, Bulgaria. The night was still very young in the early winter months of 2002 since the locals here, like in much of Europe, didn't go out to have dinner until much later in the evening. For many of the locals, the night's festivities typically began with an 8:00 p.m. dinner, lasting several hours. The dinner table, whether at one's home or at a restaurant, was always the focal point of laughter, lots of food, rich storytelling, and more laughter. Despite the hardships imposed by years of a communist system, I was always impressed by the people's ability to put it all aside and simply enjoy the moment over a meal with friends.

My work required me to liaison with law enforcement and meet "interesting" people . . . The kind of folks many of us would rather not interact with, but for my assignment, it was a must. It seemed part of some cultural requirement that many of our meetings were centered on a meal and held around a dinner table. So, with that setting, I had countless dinners, each lasting several hours, while assigned to Bulgaria. At first, given my propensity for getting things done as quickly as possible, it was a major adjustment. With time, however, I came to realize, these time-consuming endeavors were a great place to actually do my business and get things done. This emphasis on suppertime was not entirely a foreign experience for me, coming from Italian descent. I had also recently concluded a 2-year assignment to the Secret Service office in Rome, Italy, as an attaché to the American Embassy. Something, however, was different in Bulgaria. Socializing in Bulgaria involved a blend of having fun mixed with the right amount of caution.

A suspicious nature served one well in this country, regardless of the activity or surroundings you were in. The city of Sophia, as well as the country itself, is best described as a beautiful place covered by a hint of grayness. Gray is the best color I can use to describe the ever-present sentiment. It was just in the air . . . all the time, irrespective of the weather. A gray mood lurked behind every corner and could be extracted from the conversations and interactions of people, whether at work or play. I came to learn how to maneuver quite effectively in this environment, where nothing was white or black but always gray.

In general, the country had undergone changes and actually thrived despite a high level of corruption in its systems of governance. Deception with all of its consequences, especially the unintended ones, was the norm by which people experienced their day-to-day lives in Bulgaria. Despite this environment of mistrust and the sense of the unknown that characterized every encounter, I felt comfortable. I loved being "on edge"; it forced me to sharpen my senses and intuition. My days and nights in Bulgaria were, by necessity, somewhat regimented. I did my very best to remain focused on work and ensure all my personal and professional activities were devoid of routine. I made it a point to appear as if all my movements were random with no discernable pattern to the outside observer. This was due part to my training in intelligence, undercover operations, and countersurveillance techniques, but I mostly learned everything I needed in terms of survival instincts growing up in and around New York City.

Akin to riding the subways of New York as a young teenager in the 1980s, you had to have your head on a swivel and never be caught off guard, lest you be a victim of a mugging or random act of street violence. Bulgaria, in many ways, was similar, except the cost of me being off my game and becoming complacent could result in far worse consequences than having my new sneakers stolen. In this place, carelessness in one's tradecraft was not a recipe for success and could very well mean a shortened life expectancy. Contract killings were common during my time in country, and unfortunately, as in so many other places around the world, the price tag on life was cheap and always up for negotiation.

My mission in Bulgaria was straightforward as it was unique. I was to locate and apprehend a fugitive known as Petar "Peter" Simenov. Peter was a fugitive from justice and at the time, the top priority of the United States Secret Service, who wanted nothing more than his safe return to the United States to face justice. He committed federal crimes related to the distribution of counterfeit U.S. currency in the New York area, and now, I, a special agent with the Secret Service, was tasked with this important mission. Peter had been successfully investigated, charged, and arrested by Secret Service agents. However, once he was released on bail, he quickly absconded and returned to his native country of Bulgaria. I received a telephone call while in Rome from the Secret Service's Counterfeit Division. I was, let's just say, offered the assignment of tracking this fugitive—it was an "offer" I immediately accepted.

Although other Secret Service agents were on temporary assignments, I was the first agent to not only establish a permanent shop but to remain in the country for an extended period of time. I was a single man at the time and had little material possessions and binding relationships or commitments. The U.S. State Department assisted me with housing and the required paperwork to serve as an attaché to the American Embassy. Once in country, I needed to be extremely careful since my target was well connected to both the Bulgarian and Russian organized crime syndicates. If I was going to be successful in my pursuit of Peter Simenov, I needed to determine who I could trust and what networks I needed to penetrate to reach the only acceptable outcome—sending this guy back to New York City, where he would face a U.S. Magistrate judge in the Southern District of New York to answer for his crimes.

One evening, while out for an early dinner with the "crew," as I called them, which was basically my coworkers from the U.S. Embassy, an opportunity presented itself. The crew consisted of Agi, the Foreign Service national, Rob, the assistant regional security officer, and John, a fairly new career diplomat recently assigned to Bulgaria. On occasion, the station chief, Ralph, would meet us for dinner or a drink, but would usually skip the festivities that would typically follow dinner. Ralph would forego the open invitation for a very good reason. He was newly remarried and more often than not, he chose to go home to his wife, also an embassy employee. These decisions probably helped his marriage as the nightlife in Bulgaria was more geared toward a single man or one who cared little about marital vows. Ralph was absolutely fantastic. Although now retired from government service, he was a great help and provided me invaluable support and guidance.

As I reflect on it some more, it was definitely Ralph that helped me get "up to speed" as to understanding both the toxic and often dangerous political playing field in the Bulgarian underworld. He provided me the verbal playbook. A comprehensive tutorial of who's who in the Bulgarian political, social, and criminal arenas. He taught me who was who and led me toward those in government who were willing to support the United States. At times, this support was overt; most often, it took the form of a private conversation or a late-night chance encounter at some restaurant, café, or more often than not, a nightclub.

The ability to hit the ground running and know whom to work with was crucial to my mission. Prior to my full time in country, Secret Service involvement was limited, as a field agent from the Rome office would travel sporadically to Bulgaria, would work what he could for a period of 2 to 5 days, and then return to Rome. In order to be more effective in its investigative efforts and gain the full cooperation and weed out the untrustworthy Bulgarian police, a more regular Secret Service presence was required. The fact that my agency saw fit to do so was a victory, but I must admit, not planned for, by any means. It was a strategic move that proved huge dividends. I was provided temporary housing and had nothing but time on my hands, which was completely dedicated toward my work and play.

For starters, the Bulgarian police were, in many cases, an extension of the organized crime syndicates that cogoverned the country. They were not to be trusted in a wholesale fashion. Trust was to be parceled out cautiously and always subjected to a continuous vetting process. By sending me to Bulgaria full time, I was able to gain the professional trust of a select few in government and slowly worked to filling the gaps left behind when we only had a part-time presence in country. This task was not easy, and to be honest, never accomplished during my entire time in Bulgaria. Although frustrating, I understood the issues and complex environment and thus, did not take the issue personally.

I lived alone and approached everything as an opportunity to advance my work. My daily routine, although unpredictable, did have a pattern to it. I often held random meetings at various cafés and restaurants around the city. Here, I would meet with and discuss business with Bulgarian police and other government officials. More often than not, it was in these off-the-beaten-path coffee shops where I would cultivate and direct my confidential informants who came from the private and public sector and always some from society's underbelly—the criminal element. Therefore, I looked forward to my dinner with friends for the relaxation, however short-lived it provided me. Dinner usually kicked off a night out where, more often than not, I had a good time.

Since I could remember, I always ate my meals early, and in Bulgaria, I was no different. I had the culture to contend with, and through some effort and persistence, I successfully convinced my colleagues of doing the same. I argued the fact that since the restaurants would be completely empty when we arrived, we would always be guaranteed choice seating. The request for early dinner was a part of my survival instincts and plan. Again, by limiting my actions to a nonprescribed format, going against the crowd, I would better my odds of staying out of view. I also used my personal good looks to my utmost advantage.

Unlike in Italy, my dark Italian features were an oddity in Bulgaria. People were often intrigued . . . and by people, I mean mostly women. I used my looks and charm to cultivate relationships with the opposite sex, mostly romantic but not all. Many were purely professional and platonic. I enjoyed the attention and took every advantage at my disposal. I had many "friends" in key places to ensure I had a set of eyes and ears on the ground. I had my finger on the pulse of the city and exploited my status as an American diplomat, paid in U.S. dollars to treat these women respectfully, and, at times, showering them with gifts that I was easily able to afford. My network of informants and trusted female associates kept me pretty in tune with what was going on and provided me an option in the event I needed to vacate in a hurry.

Now that I convinced my friends to start the evening at an earlier time than otherwise accustomed to, I had another obstacle to overcome. This one, I readily admit, was born from a more personal interest and perhaps more desire than safety. I was a picky eater accustomed to quality ingredients made in one's own kitchen. My palate for good food filled with nutritional value stemmed from my time as a kid spent chopping vegetables, peppers, and tomatoes in my dad's deli. My time in Rome only increased my awareness of quality food. Therefore, living now in Bulgaria and not knowing a word of their language or traditions, I quickly realized I was in deep trouble.

Let me emphasis a critical point: Bulgaria was a country where deception extended itself in every part of daily life. This duplicity existed in the marketing and quality of the very food served in restaurants and sold in the markets around town. Initially, I was excited when I knew I was bound for Bulgaria in that I knew, generally speaking, their food was similar to that served in Greece and Turkey. I found this appealing and inviting. Bulgarians used lots of tomato, cucumber, and cheese salad (shopska salad), moussaka (musaka), filo pastries (byurek), and stuffed vine leaves (sarmi), much like others in Europe.

Although it all sounded fantastic and delicious, I was aware that Bulgaria was well known to the Secret Service for its penchant for fraud and deception in the counterfeiting of U.S. currency. I soon discovered their proclivity for imitation extended itself far beyond the crime of making false money. Bulgarian criminals are incredibly talented in forging almost everything, and food was no exception.

Let's take, for example, one of my favorite dishes, mozzarella cheese. Later in this book, I explain my background with this food product, having spent a good part of my childhood actually making it. In Bulgaria, mozzarella had a texture and taste that was quite peculiar. It represented a cross between having the appearance of yogurt with the taste of sharp cheddar. Not something that would be well received in any Italian restaurant back home.

At that time, and even today, there existed many documented reports where customs officials in Europe actually stopped Bulgarian truck drivers for attempting to transport spoiled meats into other countries. Much food and many brand names sold in Bulgaria were mere counterfeits, having been packaged as well-known product names, but in reality, they were just another substandard quality in disguise. Another example, although not something I enjoyed or could afford, was caviar. Bulgaria is well known for its counterfeit caviar. I was more concerned about eating substandard cheese or steak than caviar. Nonetheless, I made certain the locations I sat down to eat were safe.

One evening while out to dinner, I noticed a little Italian restaurant, just off the beaten path. Immediately upon entering and seeing the small place, sparsely decorated with part of the kitchen in view of the customers, we sat to eat and the food was not half bad. There was, however, ample room for improvement. I saw the perfect opportunity. I slowly established a relationship with the restaurant's owner, who also doubled as the chef. Together, we agreed that whenever I came to eat, he would only use locally grown products to make simple but good meals. This provided me good food from a trusted source, as well as a safe haven, of sorts, to conduct my business over dinner with friends. All of this special treatment was always followed up with a generous tip, of course.

This little eatery became my regular place to eat, even though I continued to do everything possible to avoid a regular set of behaviors. I figured I could not completely eradicate all personal risks, and at the expense of appearing routine, I chose good quality food. At dinner, our discussions primarily consisted of two topics: work and women. Sometimes, we combined them, but the default position was always women, the most interesting topic of all in Bulgaria. Bulgarian women were absolutely stunning. They exuded a level of sensuality that could easily weaken a man. For good reason, they dominated our dinner conversations. We were all single men and found the evening atmosphere both inviting and intoxicating by the radiant beauty and sexuality that Bulgarian women brought to it.

Like everything I did, there was both a reason for and a method to it. Going out for the night was no different. I prepared for the night by carefully selecting and painstakingly ironing my clothing. My attire always consisted of dark clothing, pants, and shirt underneath some sort of jacket. The jacket, whether it be my black leather one or, at times, a sport coat, served a hidden purpose. It helped to further insulate and conceal the choice location I used to hide my weapon.

In Bulgaria, like in many of my previous assignments, I made adjustments to my attire, but the only thing that remained constant was my timepiece. On my left wrist was my Rolex Submariner. This item was more status symbol than timepiece. At the time, it was the moniker of a Secret Service Special Agent. I purchased it a few years earlier while on a temporary protective assignment in support of the visit of President William Jefferson "Bill" Clinton to Sydney, Australia.

Among the rank-and-file agents, the Rolex represented a level of accomplishment. It was normally worn by agents that had completed their full-time protection assignments on the Presidential Detail. These agents having overcome all professional and personal obstacles associated with protecting the president of the United States, were offered the opportunity to purchase the watch. They sported it with great pride, knowing full well what it represented.

As a young agent, owning such a piece was a mark of accomplishment. I was always impatient. I knew the unspoken rule and cultural norm was to wait until one completed their time on the Presidents Detail to own one. I could not wait what would be at least 7 years, if not more, to have my chance. I was not going to wait until assigned to a full-time protective mission.

My desire to have this watch began during my days as a rookie agent in the New York Field Office. I saw the more senior agents wearing it, and I wanted it. Upon my return to New York from my overseas assignment to Australia I wore the watch.

I defied the norm and wore it, almost hoping people would object. It was amazing to see agents mainly from other agencies zoom in and begin to start conversations surrounding the watch and where I bought it. I loved the attention. All this came with a monetary price tag I could not afford, however. At the time, I was recently divorced and living in an attic apartment in the Bronx, all of which did not mesh with me having an expensive watch. I wanted it for what it represented within the inner circle of the agency. It was paid for with my credit card and was well worth the interest paid in late payments.

Once dressed and ready to go out, I was always overconfident. Why not? I was young, in shape, and dressed like a million bucks. There was yet another hurdle between me and the fun awaiting inside the nightclubs in Bulgaria. I had to face the selection process of gaining entry into clubs and get past the bouncers. All of the nightclubs in Sophia were staffed with menacing bouncers. These hulking men had a combination of wrestling and martial arts experience added to their bulky physics. They were very intimidating and effective at their jobs, so I thought. The bouncers physically checked club patrons for weapons prior to entering the clubs and no one ever dared challenge them.

At the time, there was a great deal of violence in Bulgaria. Turf wars in the streets of Sophia were commonplace. Anyone wearing stylish clothing or driving luxury vehicles were associated with either the Bulgarian or Russian Mafia. Unfortunately, anyone caught at the wrong place at the wrong time could end up paying the ultimate price. Finding yourself, whether by choice or bad luck, in close proximity to these Mafia folks could prove to be a fatal mistake.

In an effort to minimize the violence outside the clubs, the bouncers would physically search you. At first, whenever I planned on going to the clubs, I would avoid these pat down searches by making a pit stop and leaving my weapon at my apartment, fearing it would be discovered and taken from me during one of these searches. As time passed and the more I frequented these establishments, I evaluated how the bouncer conducted his searches. I then came up with a way to conceal my weapon based on the discernable pattern of their searches.

The men were either poorly trained and their searches sloppy or their incompleteness and failure to attention to detail was deliberate. I noticed that when a bouncer had to inspect the groin area, he displayed a hesitancy to go hands-on, so to speak. They basically avoided that area, whether it be their sense of false bravado or homophobia. I knew then how to exploit their machismo attitude. I took advantage of the fact that they were "real men" who would never dare touch or come within a safe distance from another man's most sacred place.

So I decided to test them by walking to the head of the line with a confidence bordering on arrogance. My demeanor, combined with their reluctance to search all of me, led the bouncer into believing I had nothing to hide. The first evening just prior to entering the club, I removed my Sig Sauer 230, which was a .380-caliber handgun, from my ankle holster, and placed it in my waistband. I had no holster in which to place my thin silky-looking stainless steel handgun. Rather, I positioned the weapon dead center, right over my crotch. It was a risky move at the worst and an uncomfortable one at best. If the gun moved even a bit, being unsecured, it would undoubtedly slip and fall through my pants leg, onto the floor, and at the feet of the well-dressed gorilla in front of me.

The weapon itself was absolutely beautiful. It was, in my opinion, flawless. It reminded me of the shape of the one James Bond would carry in his movies. The sexiness of the gun, mixed with my job and title, all fit together wonderfully. I was like a kid in my eagerness to catch bad guys and enjoyed the moment. I cannot tell how many women in those days held that very gun during very passionate late-night moments. It was, in some ways, like a dangerous, forbidden sex toy to some, and I played right along. Although never loaded, I am certain to have broken a rule or two in terms of allowing unauthorized access to and use of a federal firearm . . .

My actions were risky, but luckily, it turned out to be a big success! Each and every time thereafter, my sig's new home while I entered the Bulgarian club scene was in the area where my legs joined my torso! The weapon gave me what little protection a .380 would offer in a country where most of the Mafia bodyguards carried serious firepower and the use of snipers to execute contract killings quite common. The going rate to pay someone with sniper experience at this time was somewhere between 5,000 to 50,000 euros. The level of payment was dependent on how high "you" rated as a target worth killing. It was a risk-based approach to murder.

 The criminal organizations would weigh the cost of killing an individual versus the level of scrutiny or lost business public attention would garner. Unless there was a personal element or a level of perceived or actual disrespect to the criminal code of honor, I believe all contract killings were done utilizing a deliberate and thoughtful, albeit callous, decision-making process. I do not believe at that time I represented a serious enough threat or was even annoying enough to anyone to expose themselves by having me, a federal agent on a diplomatic mission to Bulgaria, killed while in country. I do believe that given my identity as a Secret Service agent and my sole purpose for being in Bulgaria, namely to locate the counterfeiting fugitive, I did gain some notoriety with the criminal element.

Dinner was now over, and my clandestine activity of slipping in and out of nightclubs in full stride. I was armed, always armed. I notice a young man, tall and blond. At first glance, I wished it were a woman based on these attributes. He was standing at a crowded bar waiting to be served. He fit the physical description of my fugitive . . . descriptors I had committed to memory. I approached the bar while he was conversing in his native Bulgarian with a beautiful woman. After a few minutes of scanning the crowd, all the while keeping him under close watch, I motioned for the bartender, another sexy woman. My God, it was difficult to remain focused in this place. I asked for a whiskey, a Jack Daniels straight up. It caught the man's attention.

He turned toward me, and I saw that he gave me a glance over but did not say a word. I did not hesitate. I said in a commanding yet subdued voice, "How are you, Peter? My name is Nino, and I work for an organization you are very familiar with . . . the United States Secret Service."

He turned away slightly, and when he faced me again after a momentary pause, obviously trying to see who was watching, he replied in perfect English, "OK and so what?" I responded with a nod and grabbed my drink and took a swig. I was never a drinker, and it tasted like jet fuel. However, under these and subsequent similar circumstances, I always ordered the same drink, regardless of whether I enjoyed it or not. Like my Rolex Submariner, it became my signature drink. I gulped the remaining contents in one stroke and immediately felt a burning sensation in my stomach. I could feel my cheeks turn red and my body temperature rise. I felt slight nauseated. What was I thinking drinking that damn whiskey so fast? I got caught up in the moment . . . *Do not get sick here, Nino, not in front of this guy.* I turned to walk away and in the strongest voice I could muster, said to Peter, "OK, then I will see you tomorrow at noon at the Borisova Gradina Park. Look for the statue of Bratska Mogila and you will find me alone."

I walked out of the club, thankfully not followed, and was able to regain my equilibrium as I caught my breath by walking a few blocks till I caught a taxi back to my apartment. While in the taxi, I called my friend Rob from the U.S. Embassy Security Office to tell him what had just happened. He had noticed the interaction but remained in the shadows of the club watching if anyone decided to follow me out. Rob offered his assistance. My nearest Secret Service backup support was located in the field offices of Rome, Italy, and Paris, France. Too far away. I needed to act fast and without delay.

I explained the plan for the next day, and he agreed to mobilize sur-veillance support while I met with Peter at the park. I was familiar with the location and the statue since I had visited Borisova Gradina Park on prior occasions. It was all prearranged as a meeting point, if, in fact, I ever made contact with Peter. The park was the ideal loca-tion where I could have a surveillance unit set up and go undetected to cover my meeting.

While I sat in the cab for the 10-minute ride back home, I felt a tremendous sense of satisfaction. My mission and sole objective for being in Bulgaria had just hit a home run. I was moving forward. I went to bed that night, excited and completely ready, knowing that the hunt for Peter had begun. With my Sig Sauer 380 tucked safely under my pillow, I immediately fell asleep with the thought of having Peter returned to justice.

2

Growing Up
Italian and the Mob

In order to gain a better understanding of who I am and an appreciation for how I managed my experiences in Bulgaria as a special agent for the United States Secret Service, it is important to know the Italian kid that grew into a young man and eventually leaped out of his family upbringing to experience life outside the norm. During my early childhood years, I lived, for a brief time, in the Bronx, New York, with my grandmother's sister Olympia in a small apartment in Mount Vernon, which bordered with the Bronx. Our apartment was on the top floor of a two-story building on Fifth Avenue over a bar called Scotty's. It was the late 1960s, and they were challenging times for my parents, Antonio and Gina, who, as a newly married Italian immigrant couple, had entered the United States in 1966.

I was born a year later on July 29, 1967, the first of three children. My brother Antonio "Tony," or Anthony, was 18 months younger than I, and my sister Rosina was 5 years younger. I was not an easy first child. In fact, I was a difficult kid, always getting into trouble at home and in school. Reflecting back on my childhood, I most likely suffered from what is now diagnosed as attention deficit disorder. I managed to escape diagnosis and medication to boot.

I remember my inability to remain focused caused me some physical pain and my parents' great concern. I was hit by cars, thankfully, slow-moving ones, on two separate occasions; once in the Bronx where my grandmother's sister lived, and then years later, in Mount Vernon, New York. In both instances, I was a pedestrian, and not paying attention to my surroundings, was struck. Perhaps I learned my lesson, as years later, my ability at paying very close attention to my surroundings and attention to details kept me safe and resulted in a few successful criminal investigations.

I was always fighting. When not yelling at or getting screamed at by my parents, I was in the middle of some street ruckus or fistfight, often the cause of which was me trying to stop some punk from bullying on someone less capable. I was a tough kid and perhaps even more stupid than tough. I have numerous scars and broken bones on my body that serve like a roadmap to this toughness and stupidity I describe.

One year, while recovering from some medical procedure on my penis that, for the life of me, I still do not know what the hell happened, I grew bored recovering in bed. So while all bandaged up and with a catheter connected to my penis, I decided it was time to go outside and light fireworks, well in advance of July 4th. I stumbled onto the street in front of my house and lit off a few M80s, not realizing that at that very moment, a Mount Vernon patrol car was turning the corner onto my block. Oh shit—I was busted red-handed. I tried, very slowly and unsuccessfully, to run up the stairs back to my bed . . . but not that day. The cop grabbed me by the arm and yanked me back. I provided some half-ass explanation that I was bored and had a tube in my dick. I remember the look on his face. It was one I would come to see often, and he was either amused or fed up with me. He let me off, so to speak, with a written warning, some made up bullshit summons. The cop, it turned out, was a regular customer at the deli, knew my parents, and I guess felt sympathy for them.

Aunt Olympia, who watched me for a short period of time as my parents sought employment, was a saint. What I remember most was her pet parrot and her homemade chicken soup. In those early years, my grandmother and great-aunt took turns caring for me while my parents worked tirelessly to gain a footing in America. Although my grandmother never spoke a word of English, she was able to hold on to a full-time job soon after entering the United States.

I remember her telling everyone how she assembled machine parts that she was tasked to do in record numbers. I don't believe Grandma ever worked an "average day" in her entire life. My mom, Gina, which was short for Luigina, and my dad, Antonio, were married in Italy, and immediately afterward, left for their honeymoon, a one-way trip to the United States with their recently awarded green card. I spent my days in the apartment as my grandmother worked the midnight shift in a factory. Mom was a seamstress by day in a sweatshop making wedding gowns, and Dad was a day laborer. This type of coming and going was the routine shift during the early years in the Perrotta household.

My childhood fantasies were filled with memories of pretending to be a cowboy who saved the day or a policeman fighting the bad guys. As I got older, these fantasies of helping those in need only grew stronger. Being initially raised in a predominately Italian neighborhood, with family members all speaking Italian, I obviously spoke Italian fluently and would get embarrassed whenever challenged to speak English.

During the 1960s, Mount Vernon was basically a divided city where many of the blacks in the South went North to Mount Vernon to get better and higher-paying jobs. The white Americans from the Bronx and Manhattan, who were escaping the high-crime rates of NYC, saw Mount Vernon as a "bedroom community," so a "white flight" ensued as well. As a result, Mount Vernon, while I was growing up, became divided in two by the New Haven Line railroad tracks of the Metro North railroad: Northside and Southside. The population south of the tracks became predominantly African American, while that north of the tracks was largely white.

Then in the late '70s, our predominately Italian neighborhood in Mt. Vernon changed dramatically. There was an influx of poor Hispanics moving into what was once Italian-dominated neighborhoods. What was once a neighborhood of storeowners and shopkeepers, all who spoke Italian, and the parish priest who also spoke Italian, was no longer the norm. In my home, since my parents were immigrants, no one spoke English at home. So with the neighborhood changing and my language barrier at school worsened by my behavior issues, I faced some serious challenges growing up. Despite these problems that lingered throughout my formal education, I knew early on that someday, I would become some type of law enforcement official.

I have fond memories of our family holiday parties where everyone, my aunts, uncles, and cousins, would get together to celebrate the day's special occasion. My family did everything together—birthday parties, holiday parties, first communions, confirmations—everything was a reason to gather in the kitchen, prepare old-style recipes, sit around the table, and eat course after course. I was the oldest child in my family, and being the oldest, I got to experience it all. I took in every aspect of a room full of Italian immigrants, the talks about the old country, American politics, sports, and, of course, the hardships of running an Italian deli.

These family gatherings were wonderful, and I cherish my memories of them . . . The delicious food, laughter, and above all, the games my cousins and I played, games that always evolved around toy guns and fireworks. I remember one morning before a family party while my parents were still asleep I wanted to see the effects of a lit firecracker and a playhouse made of plywood that I built in our basement. I placed the firecracker between two bricks propped up against the structure and lit the fuse.

The experiment was a success . . . of sorts, in that the fuse worked, there was an explosion, and the playhouse fell apart. The downside of this victory was the fact that the noise level was almost deafening, having echoed throughout our home. The firecracker went off with a resounding boom, followed by a cloud of smoke. I was so happy, but, unfortunately, my joy was short-lived.

Behind the cloud of smoke appeared my father, who, having jumped out of his bed, ran downstairs to the basement in his Fruit of the Loom white underwear with belt in hand. I got the beating of my life. Trust me, I quickly learned two lessons that morning. First, a single firecracker did not pack the necessary punch, and, more importantly, I realized my curiosity to experiment and witness the impact of an explosion would be better served outdoors.

Coming from a large Italian immigrant family, I remember being placed on the receiving end of hand-me-downs, clothing, toys, and more clothing. I hated having to wear my cousin's clothes, but I had zero input; no say. My older cousins Pete and Pat wore clothing that was in style in the late 1960s. By the time it was recycled to me, not only were they a generation behind, extremely outdated and out of style, they often did not fit well. I remember being embarrassed in school and being made fun of because of what I was wearing.

I often fought back both verbally and physically. The taunting and ridicule I was subjected to only led me to getting into more trouble and a front-row seat in the principal's office. My parents, quite frankly, had no idea how to manage me, nor the time to devote due to the demands of the deli. When I was 7 years old, my parents removed me from the public school system and placed me in a private catholic school.

The family holiday gatherings were an amazing time for me. I had an uncle who would spend the entire day getting the basement table leveled, all the while drinking his homemade wine. My uncle wanted the table perfectly situated so as not to spill a drop of the priceless homemade wine. The dinner table was a place of great respect, with every family member having his or her part to play in maintaining it as such.

Everyone in the family had a cellar that contained a homemade wine stash. I am not sure this was legal, but my family enjoyed the fruits of their homemade wine labors all throughout the year. My dad kept two 60-gallon barrels of red and one 60-gallon of white wine in our basement, all of which was consumed annually like clockwork. Once the grapes were purchased, it was only a matter of time before we crushed them, which would begin the process of fermentation.

Before we could begin the process, all of the equipment needed to be scrubbed and washed. It was a painstaking yet essential step in the wine-making process, which Nonna Luisa handled. Once everything was ready, we would prepare to crush the grapes. My father used an electric crusher, which would sit on top of this rather large wooden barrel. One by one, we (my brother and I) would begin to carry in the crates until all were thoroughly crushed. Once the grapes were crushed, they would remain in the barrels during the day.

Every night, either my father or Nonna Luisa would go down to the basement and use a long piece of wood to push the grapes down. Within a week or two, it was time to press the grapes and fill the 5-gallon glass jugs with the wine. The jugs were capped, and they would sit in the cellar. This would allow the sediment to settle to the bottom.

It has been some time since I have had an opportunity to take part in this tradition. Since the passing of my grandmother and the purchase of the family deli, this family tradition stopped, but my memories of it all have only grown as I get older. It represents a time in my life characterized by hard work but work inspired by love and familiar bonds.

As time passed, and we all became a little more American, these family parties began to dwindle. With monetary success came convenience, and with convenience came jealousy, and, sadly, a bit of arrogance. When you had very little you relied on others. The family gatherings provided me a sense of comfort and strength growing up, and to be honest, it is an experience that, looking back, I wish I could offer to my own children.

My parents provided me a lifetime of education one can never get in the finest of schools. I learned the value of honest hard work by watching them work themselves to near exhaustion, day in and day out, as they ran a 7-day-a-week business and raised three children. I learned the meaning of integrity by watching my dad always doing the right thing by Mom, by his children, and by the customers who often needed a helping hand.

Above all, I learned the true meaning of loyalty by my reflection upon their marriage. They were, and remain, extremely loyal to each other. My parents laid the groundwork to who I am today by their daily actions and, in particular, a decision they made in 1976. Although this is all great and something I cherish, the truth of the matter is also that my parents failed to pay any attention whatsoever to anything beyond the family business. The priority was always "us" working with them in some shape or form—which meant 7 days a week. When adolescence began to kick in and normal teenage angst appeared, I slowly but steadily, without falter, began to veer off the Perrotta path. This did not sit well with my mom and dad—they immediately labeled me the rebel of the family and treated me accordingly. I just wanted more out of my life. I knew I had more to give. My parents' sole desire for me was to follow in their footsteps and one day run the family business. My parents never did fully appreciate, and even today, their understanding of me is limited although their love is not.

I was 9 years old at the time and remember a buzz in the air at home. Mom Gina and Dad Antonio had just put up their entire life's savings and purchased a local deli located in Mount Vernon, New York. They were able to sacrifice and scrounge enough money over the years since arriving in America to purchase an existing business located on Gramitan Avenue in Mount Vernon, New York. Mom and Dad were able to take the next step, which had previously alluded them, and was the gold standard of all immigrants—to own your own business.

The deli was called Mercurio Delicatessen, in the heart of downtown Mount Vernon. The address was 57 Gramitan Avenue, and being a well-known location, proved to be a great investment for my parents. The deli, after a number of prosperous years, allowed us to eventually relocate to a larger location just a bit further down the block. My parents decided to acquire a three-story building that my father's brother, Mario, refurbished for them. Buying the building and owning it outright made more sense. They would never again have to pay rent to someone else. It was the American Dream.

When we transitioned, the new deli was named after the family name Perrotta. The business name was Perrotta's Salumeria. The word *Salumeria* is the Italian version of the word "delicatessen." I recall the sense of pride my dad felt but would never admit when we saw, for the first time, our family name written across the front of our business. Mom and Dad wanted people who visited to feel as if they entered an authentic Italian deli, similar to one in the old country, and his stubborn desire to keep it as such would later be the reason the business did not prosper and extend beyond one location.

In the summer of 1976, only a few weeks after the purchase, I will never forget the atmosphere in the deli. The previous owner was "Mr. Mercurio," who, days after I met him, suffered a massive heart attack. Mom and Dad were left to learn the business alone. My assignment that entire summer was to remove jars off the shelves, clean the shelves, and then restock the items. It took me the entire summer to complete the project.

At that time, there was basically 80 feet of shelving at 8 feet high. The inspection process of my work was more intense after the old owner was no longer available due to his poor health. I now had to pass a preinspection from "Nona" Luisa, only to be followed up by another inspection at the hands of my father, who was simply . . . a "hard ass on steroids." To him, nothing was ever good enough. We battled throughout my entire childhood and young adulthood on everything from the cleanliness of shelves, to politics, friends, work at the deli, to my career choices. There was never a shortage of topics my dad and I would see fit to fight over. Life was a fertile battlefield!

Looking back, I guess the fact that we were so close in proximity all the time allowed me to have this tough but very unique experience with my father, a man that believed in nothing more than hard repetitive work. He was a true workhorse. A workaholic sans diagnosis. My father enjoyed nothing more in life than a 14–16 hour workday, 7 days a week. He, followed by my mother, had neither hobbies nor interest in anything. Dad's number one fan club consisted of one diehard supporter—my grandmother and a close second, Mom.

Even on the occasions when they were at odds, and those were comical, she would praise him and criticize him in the same breath. As she put it, *"piada se mena a fatiga pa faca!"* When loosely translated from Old Neapolitan dialect to modern English, it basically means he loved work so much, if allowed, he would throw the work all over his face. An action, if you need clarity, is similar to what a pig does with food. I usually took this as my cue for me to argue, and, of course, it was followed up with some sort of discipline from either my mom and/or dad since it would typically get out of hand.

Honestly, I worked at the family business, was very good at it, but hated it with a passion. I was good at dealing with people and had a knack with the customers. I demonstrated an aptitude for cooking. However, I mean, really, like all children, I often fantasized and let my imagination run wild and had nowhere to play it out. With no options available, I frequently did this while working at the deli. I pictured myself working far away from the deli aisles, and when I told people what I wanted to be when I grew up, the deli was never factored in.

By the time I was 12 years old, I had a key role in making the mozzarella cheese while my younger brother Antonio mastered the sausage production piece of the operation. Everyone worked at the deli, including my grandmother. In addition to cleaning up at the store, she helped all of us as a secondary hand wherever needed; she would cook all the meals for the deli customers to include the catering ordered then clean the house, wash our clothing, and, of course, help watch over the three children if one got sick.

My grandmother was a saint, basically raising my siblings and me during our early years. I never saw someone work so hard with so much joy. Truly inspiring. As my brother and I grew older, everyone reported to work. Almost everyone, but my sister was somewhat protected from the workload my brother and I had to endure. If I close my eyes, I can still visualize those days, lovely days when everyone was behind the counter with Mussolini—I mean my father.

My mother was a tremendous salesperson who never studied marketing or read a business book. She was a natural. On occasions, she would catch me staring at her as she engaged with customers. It was something to see how she would very methodically lure the customer into a conversation about a particular type of cheese or cut of meat. She would sprinkle this dialogue with stories of her childhood back in Italy—all centered around how fresh and delicious the meals were. Once they were hooked, Mom would, with a quick, subtle turn, look at me and wink. Her smile would tell me that she got them, and she knew it! She made the sale!! These are very meaningful recollections I have of my mother. The memories, although faded a bit over time, are as significant to me now as were those stolen unspoken moments so long ago between a young boy and his mother. These were great times, even formidable ones, and above all, they represent an unforgettable period in my life for which I am ever grateful.

It is important to know that my parents made the deli their entire life's purpose. We all had to work there; there was no option to the contrary. My brother Antonio was 18 months younger than I, and my sister Rosina was 5 years younger. The thought of participating in organized sports and even doing schoolwork was placed in a far distant second to our obligations at the deli. As the oldest child, I obviously was expected to work harder, and more was expected of me.

However, as we grew and were able to help out, our responsibilities increased accordingly. We received recognition and were rewarded based upon on how hard we worked for our parents. We all worked extremely hard, and I absolutely hated it. The Perrotta deli, for me, was basically as Dante in *The Inferno* would call a "tragedy." I loved soccer and hated school since school work it did not come easy for me.

I entered elementary school speaking fluent Italian and had a poor command of the English language. The neighborhood in which I was raised was made up of primarily Italian immigrants. No one spoke English. I was held back in first grade, and then had great trouble with math and English my entire school experience, basically because of my inability to speak fluent English. School did not come easy for me, and most of the time, I either copied from other students or just failed.

On occasions, I would have a little spurt of productivity and success. Looking back, I think I was too tired from working; therefore, developing studying skills just never happened. On the other hand, what did happen was that from an early age, through the deli, I became a businessman. I quickly absorbed the art of negotiating by dealing with stubborn sales reps and satisfying difficult clients.

I had many responsibilities at the store, which I shared with my brother Anthony. One such job was to watch patrons and deter those few who would come in and attempt to steal food products and merchandise.

As I grew older and stronger, my other job was one, which, at times, was quite enjoyable. I had to occasionally redirect the drunks and the mentally ill out of the store. Since I had a passion for law enforcement, I actually enjoyed these duties.

Whenever the Mount Vernon police came in for a sandwich or a sampling of some food my mom and dad were selling, I would stare at their uniform, badge, and gun. I would often engage them and share my experiences with the neighborhood delinquents. They always told me the same thing: do not intervene, stay away, and let the police handle it. On the other side of the counter, there was my mom, a master at satisfying clients, and dad, a master at business. We had great instructors. After watching my interactions with the police, my dad always reminded me that I was just "wasting his and my time."

We worked in the heart of downtown Mt. Vernon, about 25 miles from New York City. Mt. Vernon, at the time, was a city whose ethnic traditions were slowly but steadily being fused with the influx of other cultures. African, Brazilian, and Portuguese now dominated what were once Jewish, Italian, and Irish neighborhoods. The influence of these new cultures had a great impact on our business. New cultures equated to different interests in food and grocery products. Another challenge to our livelihood was the fact that the business was flanked by two strip clubs.

The people surrounding these clubs, as well as those who operated them, are typically associated with organized crime. One character I recall vividly was the owner of one of the clubs. "Tony" was his name. He was a short but stocky man in his early 40s. To a kid, it seemed old at the time. He looked like he lifted weights at one point and focused primarily on his chest and bicep muscles. Tony wore a dark wig which looked out of place and unnatural, but who would dare call him out about it? One thing was certain . . . Tony was very street savvy, and a quality one can only get by living in certain inner-city environments. In keeping with all stereotypes, Tony was indeed connected with certain elements of the criminal underworld. He spent a great deal of time and money in the deli.

I found Tony intriguing and immediately gravitated to him, if only from afar. He wore black pants, black shirts and lots of gold chains and a pinky ring all the time. In the summer, they were tight T-shirts made of silk material, and in the winter, he wore a thin custom-fit black leather jacket. When he paid for his purchases, he would pull out a wad of crisp 100-dollar bills from his front pocket, often referred to as a "C" note. My father loved Tony because of the money he spent in the business. He purchased large chunks of Parmigiano-Reggiano cheese, dry sausage, and provolone cheese on a weekly basis. One day, Tony came in with his Filipino girlfriend, an ex-stripper, and asked Dad to cut him a piece of provolone cheese. Of course, this request made my father very happy. Dad walked to the rear of our deli, pulled out a 4-foot long wedge of well-aged "Auricchio" provolone, and started by placing his large knife on the wedge ready to cut a 1-inch thick piece.

Tony stopped him with a mere facial expression, so Dad moved the knife for a wider wedge. As Tony continued to signal with just his demeanor and a slight squint of his eyes, my father became visibly and steadily happier. The chunk of cheese that was eventually cut was a very impressive one and quite expensive. My dad began to push down on the knife blade, and Tony was flirting with his girlfriend, only to be interrupted briefly by Mom who handed them both a sample of the cheese for their tasting. The deli was typically, and perhaps not coincidentally, empty whenever Tony entered. I think he preferred it that way. Regardless, my father always seemed pleased when Tony walked in because his purchases were always substantial, and more importantly, Tony never questioned the bill.

Tony was obviously connected in some way to organized crime, and word on the street was that he had local politicians in his pocket. If you needed a loan or you wanted to place a bet on your favorite team, Tony and his associates were the ones you needed to see. In the summer months, he and other similar-looking men would stand outside the strip club and lean against new Cadillacs and discuss business. The entire experience was so intriguing to me at the time, and it not only ignited my interest in, but helped shape my understanding and approach to, the underworld.

Because of my family dynamics, the deli served, for all purposes, the role of "our home" and "our playground," where we grew up, and in the case of my brother and me, got into trouble. My sister Rosina, being the baby of the three children, experienced less of what my brother and I did. I will never forget one Sunday morning, I decided to grab a dozen eggs, climb up to the roof through an attic access point with my scared brother, and began to throw eggs at every storekeeper in my field of vision.

I specifically trained my sights on an all-men's clothing store across the street. The front door was covered in eggs as was the Cadillac convertible parked in front of my dad's place. There were eggs all over the front driver's seat. It didn't take long for me to become the prime suspect. What my parents lacked was proof until my grandmother, Nona Luisa, found the half-empty carton of eggs tucked behind the row of eggs for sale in the rear frig. My dad gave me what, in the neighborhood, was called a "shellacking."

My parents were busy working and never had time for anything but work, and basically, as long as we were not getting into trouble, we were left to our own devices. We were free to make our own decisions when it came to "higher" education. When it was time to pick a high school, I selected Archbishop Stepinac, White Plains, New York, despite the fact that most of my close friends went to other high schools. At the time, I selected Stepinac since it had a great soccer team, and I loved soccer! Whenever I could, I would play soccer at the expense of making my father angry since it took me away from working at the deli. Soccer was one of my great passions as a child, as was becoming a federal agent.

I was a goalkeeper and practiced often. During a high school season, my father pulled me from attending a very important semifinal game. My team lost the match. As the starting goalkeeper for the varsity team, my absence did not go over well with my coaches and teammates. They blamed the loss on me and paid me back by banning me from the high school yearbook. Most teens I knew would have gone into a bout of depression due to this level of social outcasting. I was angry at my father. He wanted to hear none of it.

I internalized my feelings and turned it into a positive experience. The following year, I ran for class president and won. I then ran for school president but was initially informed by the school dean that my grades were not acceptable for such a position. I challenged him respectfully and was eventually granted permission to continue my campaign for school president. I won the election and never looked back! One thing clients at the deli, friends, and family members will admit to this day . . . once I put my mind to something, I often succeeded.

So having worked for Mom and Dad my entire childhood and teenage years of life, as I grew older, I needed money to buy the things I wanted, the things my dad would always consider a waste of time and money. On occasions, whenever possible, I worked as a waiter to make some additional income in between shifts at the deli. I remember my salary at the deli. My father, who I called *babbo*, which means "dad" in Italian, only paid me $50 a week. At the age of 10, $50 was like a million dollars. However, at the age of 17, $50 a week was something, sure, but I was now dating and wanted to have gas and spending money. The money I made was used to take little trips with friends, and it was used to purchase the things that I wanted. I felt good about myself, and although I always had to be on call to work at the deli, as I began to make money outside the deli, I began to further explore the real world outside the confines of my parents' food business.

We were always saving. My parents were disciplined in their approach to money and would always err on the side of thriftiness when faced with an option. I understood this philosophy during the early years. There was a time we went 3 years in a row where we couldn't afford a Christmas tree. None of kids dared complained. The Perrotta propaganda machine was a force to be reckoned with as well as effective and convincing. We all fell into formation. That, of course, all changed once we were teenagers . . .

My first full-time job not working for my parents started at Citibank. I worked at a call center in White Plains, New York. The office was a call center where we would answer the calls from mostly existing customers. At first, I worked evening shifts by basically cold-calling existing customers about their bank accounts and asking general customer care questions. I was a natural salesman but wanted absolutely nothing to do with banking.

So, at first, the supervisors were all over me: "Perrotta, please see me in my office." They would start by saying something like "so we monitored your last call and you are totally off script." My response was always very apologetic mixed with a genuine yet feigned concern. I would then promise to follow the script—yet, inside me, I wanted to say, "Hey, do you really understand the customers' concerns? If so, why are we redirecting them to what we want to talk about?"

My goal with every call was for the customer to be completely satisfied with their request, and the script provided none of that; it lacked appreciation and understanding of their needs. The center's true goal was totally geared into ramming more bank products down the client's throat. Selling people products they did not need was not for me.

My life experiences garnered from the family business taught me that by listening to the client and their needs in the long run, you not only had a repeat client but also one who would listen to you when you had something to say. My dad, when he spoke, which was only on rare occasions, resulted in increased purchases by the customer. Mom talked about everything the client wanted to talk about. She always led the family in sales. It seemed as if people couldn't stop buying when she was around.

I applied those techniques to my clients at Citi, and they eventually made a difference. After a few months of almost constant coaching, reprimands, and almost getting fired, something happened. The sales manager in charge of the whole center looked at the quarterly statistics and realized something. I, the new kid on the block, with no formal sales training and a totally unorthodox approach to dealing with Citibank customers, led the office in sales, had the most satisfied clients, and above all, received tremendous positive clientele feedback.

I now became the icing on the 1-800-Citi call center cake . . . Soon afterward, the ridged scripts were thrown away and the free-flowing approach was introduced to the floor. Of course, you needed to be somewhat on point, but the ridged approach went out the door, and so did I since I was waiting for the U.S. Army top-secret clearance to be completed, and then to give me my reporting date to Fort Huachuca, Arizona.

These were not easy times for me. Although very difficult and not without consequences, I basically turned my back on my father's wishes of taking on the family business or something very similar. But rather by me joining the military while in college and setting my goals on pursuing a career in law enforcement, I defied the patriarch of the Perrotta family, and in some ways, broke my mother's heart. Today, I now understand my dad's reservations as these career choices did not demand respect or pay well in Italy. Although I tried desperately to gain his approval, to no avail, I had made my move, and they had made theirs.

3

The Jackass Meets Elmer Fudd

My law enforcement break had finally come. It's the early 1990s in New York, and things seem to be moving in the right direction. I had not long ago graduated from Fordham University, armed with a bachelor's degree in political science and a minor in philosophy. I was newly married to a woman I met at Fordham, and I had successfully completed a 6-month U.S. Army Military Intelligence Officer's Basic Course at Fort Huachuca, Arizona. Even back then, I knew that any one of these milestones, let alone the combination of them, were cause enough to pause and celebrate.

I, however, chose not to do so. Looking back now over a distance brought upon by over a quarter-of-a-century timespan, what excited me the most was not having fallen in love and marrying my beautiful young bride. Nor did becoming the first in my family of hardworking Italian immigrants to earn a college degree in the United States quite do it for me. What made me happy was the fact that I applied, and secured, a probationary position as an investigator with the Bronx District Attorney, Detective Investigator (DI) Squad. The day I received my letter in the mail advising me to report to the Rockland County Police & Public Safety Academy filled me with a sense of pride and level of satisfaction unknown to me previously. Finally, I was on my way to my coveted place in law enforcement.

I needed, for the next 6 months, to report daily to the police academy located in Pomona, New York. It was a quaint location and far cry from the streets where I grew up. My commute to the academy was about an hour's drive each way from my one-bedroom apartment in Riverdale, New York. At the time, my wife and I chose to live in Riverdale since it helped me meet the residency requirements of my new job. We also picked Riverdale, a section of the Bronx that was close to both Westchester County where our family and friends lived, and it was also an easy commute over the George Washington Bridge to New Jersey where her parents lived.

The police academy physical requirements were not difficult. I was in excellent physical shape and the written exams, although you needed to listen in class, were geared to have us all pass. I attended the academy with two other candidates who were also to report to the Bronx DI Squad. With the exception of the three of us, everyone else in the academy was to start as a uniformed patrolman in one of the numerous police departments located throughout the state of New York. I was excited, and each day at the academy, I felt a surge go through my body. It was a mix of excitement and a sense of accomplishment. I mean—wow!—I am almost there, and this position was going to be the one that will get me to my last stop—the one that would allow me to finally become a federal agent!

I was very excited to see my career in law enforcement moving forward. Soon, I would be handling cases in the Bronx as an investigator with full police authority. I focused on further developing my investigative skill sets all to better prepare me for the day I eventually took on the Mafia. My goal was set, and I had my eye on the target, becoming a famous investigator of Italian heritage and fight those who swore allegiance to Cosa Nostra. As I reflect, now this seems so distant from our current needs. As terrorism today has taken center stage and the threat environment has drastically changed since the September 11 attacks, we hardly hear about the Mafia nor law enforcement's efforts to fend off these evildoers. Instead, "ISIS" has become a household word. What a change. America has changed.

As I described in an earlier chapter, these investigative skills were first honed in my childhood and practiced during my young adult life in the family-owned business. All the skills a good investigator needs, I learned behind the counter in my parents' deli—observation, interaction with the public, negotiation with customers, anticipating people's needs, and identifying their weak spots and motivations.

I also earned an invaluable education in that store, one no textbook can impart nor an academy class adequately convey. I had a front-row seat, up close and personal, to real-life wise guys. They came in and out of my parents' store with such regularity, that the colorful language they used and the animated way in which they carried themselves became commonplace for me. I saw and heard their interactions and witnessed them during some unguarded moments as they ordered specialty food items and just conversed with each other while waiting for my dad to slice the mortadella. I saw and heard these Mafiosos operate in plain view. I took it all in and was fascinated with every minute of the show. It helped shape how I eventually carried myself and operated as a "mob buster."

My real-life experience only complimented the technical training received both in the army and at the police academy. At Fort Huachuca, my investigative skills underwent a bit of analytical peppering during my initial military basic training, and later, I underwent a "deep dive" in the analytical thinking emphasized at the U.S. Army Military Intelligence Counterintelligence School. After receiving my commission as a second lieutenant in the United States Army Reserves, December 1990, while attending graduate school, I took an educational delay option and reported to Fort Huachuca in January 1992. There in Fort Huachuca, while struggling with the overwhelming information and rigid classroom structure, I was presented with a difficult situation, a leadership challenge that was obviously not part of the formulized training.

A female classmate who was a West Point graduate became a close friend. She was married to an army Special Ops lieutenant who was in the Middle East at the time. One evening while out returning to her apartment, she was taken advantage of and raped by the class coordinator. The class coordinator, a fellow lieutenant, was also part of the training staff, and had allegedly previously done the same horrific act of violence when he attended West Point. Now, this criminal in uniform, having been expelled from West Point previously, still managed to get an Officer Candidate School (OCS) commission.

So after completing his OCS training, years later, this degenerate shows up as an instructor, and we were the unfortunate class to have him. My friend contacted me early in the morning and was distraught. All I heard was her crying and muttering a few words of what was done to her. I immediately ran over to her barracks and after much encouragement, persuaded her to go to the hospital. The poor woman was traumatized, had been subjected to a horrific act, and was concerned about what her husband was going to think. What a difficult situation to be forced into through no fault of her own. As she was being examined, I reported the incident to the lieutenant's commanding officer, the captain in charge of him and my class of recruits.

It was difficult decision as I weighed the consequences of reporting our superior officer. This was akin to being a whistleblower but without the protection afforded them under the usual reports of government waste, fraud, and abuse. I knew this call needed to be made, I needed to make it happen, and I did. After my notification, formal United States Army investigative procedures and protocols ensued. Things were precarious in the unit for a while. Tension mounted as sides were drawn and assumptions made as to guilt. However, in time, justice was served, and things got back to normal. I often wondered how my friend functioned under her new normal and the horrendous situation in which she was forced to cope.

Upon the completion of my military training, notwithstanding my less-than-stellar performance rating, I was able to land an investigator job. I was hired by the Civilian Complaint Review Board (CCRB) for the city of New York. At the CCRB, I was one of the very first civilian investigators hired under a new initiative to replace police investigators. The CCRB was removed from the authority of the New York Police Department by then Mayor David Dinkins. Known as the former New York Police Department Civilian Complaint Investigative Bureau, the CCRB was now slated to emerge into a more independent agency. This was all done in response to the tremendous public outcry over racially charged incidents in and around the city as well as complaints of excessive abuse of police authority. One such incident in the city's history which itself has been topic of much debate served as a catalyst for this change, the Crown Heights riots.

I now worked in the investigative unit of an independently controlled and newly led civilian organization. All of us CCRB investigators had subpoena authority which was paramount to any chance of building strong cases that would stand up to a multitude of scrutiny, both internal and external, to the department. We had the ability to recommend disciplinary measures in cases where allegations of police misconduct were substantiated. I jumped in with both feet and soon investigated cases involving public allegations against officers of the New York Police Department (NYPD). These accusations centered on charges of abuse of force, discourtesy, offensive language, and abuse of authority.

As a new investigator, I needed to ensure I was well versed on both the law and facts surrounding each case. As someone tasked with interviewing sworn officers of New York's Finest, the need to be prepared was an understatement. Added to the pressure I felt as a rookie was the presence of Police Benevolent Association (PBA) representatives at all officer interviews. PBA representation, itself both necessary and worthwhile, did, at times, prove a hindrance to seeking justice both for the public and, in many instances, for the cops themselves.

There are subtle differences between the investigation of a civilian and that of a police officer brought to the CCRB. The commonalities all reside in the constitutional rights to which all citizens are entitled. What I refer to are the differences in practice. Typically, when a member of the public is interviewed and/or investigated, initially, unless otherwise requested, legal representation is normally not on hand. Furthermore, little to no information is usually shared by the investigator. These types of investigations are very much a "one-sided" deal.

However, this interaction was not the case with CCRB investigations of the NYPD. The officer in question had time to review the complaint and discuss it with his/her PBA representative prior to the interview. This was the equivalent of giving the opposing team your playbook before the big game. So being poorly prepared was not an option as it only further limited any chance of gaining additional clues or investigative leads from the interview. It was like a championship chess match in its penchant for deliberate thought, use of strategy, and evaluation of one's opponent—but much different. This was not a game. It represented serious consequential issues, and the stakes were much higher.

I was already equipped with the basic building blocks and necessary investigative tools to be successful at the CCRB. The essential ingredients of any good investigator were embedded into my DNA from the exposure I had at the family business since 90 percent is having good communication skills. So I always began by putting the police officers that I was about to interview at ease. For very good reasons, they always entered my interview rooms filled with tension, apprehension, and often, downright hostility. I found that by simply walking into the room with a genuine smile on my face and acting in a professional, respectful, and extremely pleasant manner, the walls always seemed to drop just enough to allow me a peek onto the other side.

My recipe for getting people to talk was rather simple, yet, many could never come to master it. I always treated the officers and their PBA representatives with the respect they deserved, regardless of the accusations that brought them to my doorstep. The key to any human interaction, in my opinion, is authenticity. I was always genuine in both my civility and in my anger. When dealing with professionals, whether they be in my same line of work, law enforcement, or with the career criminal, contrived emotion will always be sniffed out immediately.

I learned early on that a certain level of shrewdness could be masked with a refined and mannerly approach. I began, conducted, and ended all my interviews with a level of curiosity that teetered to, and from varying degrees of, intensity, but never died out. All successful people are curious, always seeking more, looking into the unknown. The same applied to my investigations early on in my career. I would begin by gently asking a question, careful not to offend or alarm, only to come back to it later several times over.

This would normally result in the person becoming confused and disoriented as to what they said, when they said it, and to whom they said it. When the answers didn't make sense, I would politely ask for forgiveness and continue probing for clarity, always working to keep them comfortable, careful to maintain the perceived balance of power. I employed this tactic throughout my entire career, and it really worked well for me whenever I had an important interview.

For instance, at the CCRB, it lulled the officers who had something to hide into a false sense of comfort. By my systematic yet disarming line of attack, it was not until way down the road that the guilty would go off script, often saying more than what was previously advised by counsel, only to realize it was too late. On many occasions, the PBA representative would shake their heads or tug on the officer's sleeve to prevent them from saying another ill-spoken word. More often than not, it was too little too late.

The tape recorder, like an elephant in the room, could not be missed. There it was, placed dead center on the table, between myself and them. It recorded every word, every subtle innuendo, question, denial, and stall tactic, but it always captured the information, unfiltered and raw. I always left the interrogation rooms as I entered them, with a big smile. I would thank everyone as I collected my evidence and walked out. Sometimes, my smile was more genuine, more heartfelt, and bigger depending, of course, on what was caught on tape.

I was not in the business of going after cops—I wanted to get to the truth. I would conduct myself in the same way and utilize similar investigative ploys against civilians whose sole motivation was to use the CCRB as a means by which to deter and defame an active and honest cop. I had a knack for detecting these phonies and would immediately and effectively put an end to their ill thought out scheme.

I remember a specific case where officers assigned to the NYPD plainclothes street crime unit were getting slammed with CCRB complaints. The two officers, Billy Dentrone and Erick Hendricks, were some of the most dynamic, sincere, and reliable cops I had the pleasure of meeting during my time at CCRB. After interviewing these two dedicated public servants, separately, of course, I realized that they were honorable men who were truly trying to fight crime and protect the public. I pursued every opportunity to collect the information and develop the evidence I needed to prove the case filed against them was simply retribution from the criminal whom they had previously arrested. In order to do this, though, I had a major problem to overcome. Talk about a wall. I not only needed a peek at the other side, I actually needed the wall knocked down, if only temporarily.

I needed copies of the officers' memo book entries and other pertinent documents that the PBA representative advised them, under no circumstances, were they to provide to me. This was standard procedure on the part of the PBA, and it made absolute sense in many respects. The PBA representative knew that by excluding the written information from the formal CCRB investigation, he would generally protect the officers from potential inconsistencies written in their daily log. Thus, by playing it safe and denying such requests, the PBA did, in fact, make it more difficult to prove their clients' guilt. However, on the other hand, they also made it more unlikely the officers' innocence would be demonstrated.

A CCRB investigation that resulted in the determination of "no information," one way or the other, would be considered simply a complaint that was not substantiated. An unsubstantiated claim, in the eyes of the PBA, was, in fact, a victory. I wanted the truth, and in the case of these two officers, I knew it was more than just a PBA statistical, play-it-safe win. I knew these men were accurate and honest in their written reporting based on the flow of details they each provided me during their initial interviews.

I remember meeting them one afternoon on the upper level of the Brooklyn Bridge to elicit valuable information and details that would eventually be used to exonerate these men and put the case where it belonged. I came with a genuine spirit of trying to do the right thing by these two cops. Now, I needed to convince them to trust me with their careers, and in some respects, their very lives. I came to find out that Billy Dentrone trusted me from the very beginning when our paths crossed at the initial intake at the CCRB. Coincidentally, he and I have, in recent years, reconnected and I consider him a very dear friend. Billy's partner, Erick Hendricks, on the other hand, was not so trusting, and understandably, a bit hesitant to believe in me. It made complete sense when you think about it. I was a civilian employee, selected by the mayor's office, with the directive to investigate cops.

This still smells of politics and sounds like the prerequisites to be a bus driver. Because that is how I was often viewed—as the guy who would not only throw you under the bus, but drive it over you a few times for good measure. Given this description of my job duty, would you trust me or any CCRB investigator? It took some doing, but after a while, Erick came to realize and saw firsthand that in the end, my sole intention was to do the right thing by him and his partner; namely, to clear their good names. He and I also reconnected years later and remain trusted friends.

I made much headway that day as we discussed their case overlooking the beautiful Manhattan skyline. In short time, they agreed and provided me their daily logbooks against the advice of the PBA. I remain grateful to these men for taking a huge leap of faith and placing their trust in me, a young man and novice investigator. In return, I delivered exactly what I promised. I used their own written entries to help prove their innocence.

These men, along with their fellow police officers, were on the front lines in the fight against crime. This fight often played out on city streets, in an urban landscape that was very easy to ignore from the safety and distance of the suburbs. Life in New York City during this time was far more dangerous than it is today due to the very efforts of the NYPD. Life as seen from their eyes took on a different meaning, and it was my willingness to genuinely see it from their perspective that made me realize, they only wanted what was best for both the city and its law-abiding citizens.

The decisions I made and actions I took at CCRB were ingrained in me from an early age. I grew up in a family that mistrusted the police in American because of the reputation the police had back in their country. They did, however, believe in being truthful, following the law and contributing to society with hard work. My family were people who firmly believed in commitment. Therefore, regardless of their mistrust in figures of authority, they did, however, appreciate those who displayed unyielding devotion to a higher cause. I was now ready to dive into my career as a criminal investigator and within a short period of time, my next move up the career ladder was within reach.

To be clear, the traditional NYPD entity assigned to the district attorney's office was commonly referred to as the "DA" Squad, not be confused with the Detective Investigator (DI) Squad. The DA Squad was considered to be the primary investigative unit and given priority by the department in all things funding, equipment, and cases. The DA squad was typically staffed by career NYPD officers; actually, detectives. These detectives were comprised of two types; either top-tier seasoned veterans that earned their detective shields by making great cases or those detectives that did not. This group was assumed to have a huge "hook" at One Police Plaza, thereby guaranteeing them the coveted position absent the requisite years and hard work put in by others.

I actually relished being a member of the less-regarded DI Squad. I considered it to be a mere extension of me as it served my purposes and was a great fit with my personal style and demeanor. I sought to stand out among the acceptable level of mediocrity surrounding me by hard work, honesty, and grit. I subjected myself to the all-too-often whims and outbursts of supervisors who had not a clue on how to manage programs, work cases, or lead people. I knew that, in time, I would be a leader and prepared myself every day for when such an opportunity presented itself.

The DI Squad was poorly respected among the established law enforcement entities and, at best, a cause for confusion as to its mission, purpose, and jurisdiction among the various assistant district attorneys. For my part, I was never confused. I knew my mission and understood my purpose very clearly. Despite the organization for which I worked, I was respected by my counterparts and treated fairly. It was also becoming clearer to me that the path forward to become a mob buster was becoming a reality. The road I needed to travel was slowly beginning to appear in my front sights. I had my course set. I assumed the path toward organized crime fighting would consist of many miles and take many years to traverse. I imagined myself taking on the head of a crime family after having worked many high-profile cases and achieving supervisory rank within the federal law enforcement profession. Neither could be further from the truth. My break was going to come soon enough!

I never played or bought into office politics, a nuance that I am sure played a factor in my career years later. I simply worked very hard all of the time. I avoided social gatherings, happy hours, and the long, seemingly never-ending squad lunches. I viewed all of this as a waste of time, and I had none to waste. I wanted to go after the mob and was in a rush to do it. I was like my father in many ways; this was no different. He was a no-bullshit kind of a guy. Antonio Perrotta believed in a simple life but had a solid understanding that dedication to work and his family were essential and nonnegotiable. He was not there to make things easy on people, placate feelings, or support anything outside of the family business.

Looking back, I wonder who I would be as a man and where I would be in my personal and professional life, had I experienced a different upbringing. Maybe I would not have been so hard on myself, and perhaps would have taken the time to really enjoy life and my accomplishments. Or quite possibly, I would have turned out like so many kids from my neighborhood . . . involved in a life of crime and dead ends. Growing up, I was a tough kid who did not fear anyone. This attitude without the firm hand of my father could have easily led me into the wrong lifestyle. A life completely opposite of the one I chose.

My life was changed forever on a day that was nonmemorable other than for the fact that I was summoned into the chief's office. Upon entering the office, the chief of the Bronx District Attorney, Detective Investigator Squad, I vividly recall first noticing his deputy chief who will also remain unnamed, seated adjacent to the chief's desk. He was staring at the floor. I found this odd, I guess, as it still is fresh in my memory. The meeting was brief and strange, but it is one I will never forget. In that meeting, the chief, who looked and acted like the cartoon character Elmer Fudd, said to me, "We have a case, kid; lots of issues up there in White Plains, but, uh, we have a joint case with them, and it is a serious Mafia case." Although he sounded ridiculous, lacked clarity, and his deputy chief added not a single word to the conversation, I was insanely thrilled and honored by it.

Just like that! I had been tasked to report to OCTF, which was located in White Plains, New York. Never mind that my assignment was billed as a low-level Mafia gambling case with no prospects or legs, as was the common jargon in the field. It was my second month on the job, and here I am, walking in to my boss's, boss's boss, wearing no jacket, my Beretta 9 mm gun snug in my new shoulder rig just like I imagined it to be as a child. In between mopping the floors and prepping the vegetables at my dad's deli, I would often daydream of one day wearing the shoulder rig with a semiautomatic pistol and matching handcuffs at my side. Just like the ones worn by the cops on TV. Actually, I wore my handcuffs in the lower part of my back for easy reach, and it looked cool, so I thought. The shoulder rig was made by a company called Galco and was very popular among law enforcement types. The shoulder gear was known as the "Jackass" rig.

It came with tie-down clamps, which I refused to use because, well, they just didn't look cool. You never saw Crockett and Tubs wear tie-downs as they chased drug dealers or drove down the strip in my favorite TV show, *Miami Vice*. So there I was, brand-new, looking good in my own mind, and sitting in his office. It was awkward, to say the least. The chief, sitting there in his big chair staring at me from top to bottom, scratching his head and not saying a word. He then began to explain how important it was for me to take this next assignment seriously.

Seriously? I needed to be serious? Was it my jackass rig or my constant smile that made him believe I needed to be serious? I thought to myself . . . Anyway, in that meeting, I was told to report OCTF within the week. I closed out all my remaining cases, cleared my makeshift desk, and enthusiastically reported to White Plains, New York, the home of OCTF's headquarters, ready to hit the ground running!

Reflecting back, I was a bit confused about the reason behind this transfer. There were many senior investigators in the DI Squad. Ones who were far more seasoned than I and had made some great arrests and successfully closed complex investigations. In my favor, though, was youth, exuberance, and some success in having developed confidential informants, located witnesses, and closed cases. In a very short period, I developed a reputation for doing good quality work despite occasionally pissing people off. I experienced some ridicule, and was, at times, ostracized by those civil servants who saw my aggressive work ethic as a threat. I did not appeal to a culture that was content and actually stuck in doing the bare minimum.

I later learned that the chief had previously assigned other DIs to White Plains to work the very same joint case. These veterans were all dismissed from OCTF for reasons related to poor performance and downright incompetence.

The assistant district attorney (ADA) in charge of the case to which I was newly assigned was named Vincent Heintz. Vincent was a tough prosecutor from the Bronx District Attorney's Office. The lead investigator was from OCTF, a retired NYPD sergeant named Echo Gaudioso. Echo became a mentor to me, and we developed a bond that exists to this day. These men impressed me immediately as no-nonsense professionals who I came to learn, later on, never suffered fools lightly.

So the chief, who had no one left in the bullpen, his reserves empty, reluctantly assigned me to the case. Basically, neither he nor his deputy could handle me. Both men were career city government employees and built most of their law enforcement careers in the DI Squad. They were not comfortable with someone with my over-the-top personality hanging around the office. My personality, I later learned, often did not mesh well with and among the typical law enforcement folks I came into contact with over the next 2 decades. I must admit though, I thoroughly enjoyed the work at the DI Squad and among the laziness, I discovered a few characters within their ranks. It was a great place to learn investigative work, and I remain grateful for having had the opportunity to have been among their ranks, however brief a stint it was.

Now, exactly how I got to the Bronx Detective Investigative Squad all occurred with a late-night conversation in Germany. I was on a 2-week active reserve duty assignment in Augsburg, Germany. Chief Warrant Officer Edward "Eddie" Mangano, who was also a First-Grade Detective for the NYPD, took me under his wings. I was a young second lieutenant fresh from completing my training. Eddie took a liking to me. After working alongside him for 2 weeks, Eddie made a call to a family member who was an assistant district attorney supervisor for the Bronx County District Attorney's Office. Just like that, with one telephone call and an act of kindness, I was asked to report to the Bronx DA for an interview shortly after my return from Germany.

I will never forget how Eddie took a chance on me. He gave me my first real break in law enforcement. Soon after my initial interview with senior supervisors at the DA's office, a background investigation followed, and within 2 months from the date of my first interview, I received my notice to report to the Rockland Police Academy. My path to doing what I dreamed about was slowly coming together. I prepared for my time at the police academy, all the while having also applied to several federal law enforcement agencies. All in an effort to hedge my bets and always be in a position to fulfill my ultimate goal—to become a federal agent fighting organized crime! All I needed to do was continue working hard and prove my worth to the task at hand. When opportunity came to knock, it need not bother—my door would be wide open!

It was December 1995, and I would soon be gone from the OCTF as the United States Secret Service had sent me an acceptance letter offering me conditional employment. My pace did not let up as I was now fully engaged in my temporary assignment at the OCTF. I had begun to lay the groundwork to what would eventually become the biggest case of my career, the case against the Gambino crime family. As Christmas drew near, I continued working feverishly on a case that had been previously launched a few years prior. I put in very long days and nights into this case, mulling over case files and reviewing unknown amounts of evidentiary items, learning and looking for clues.

Unbeknownst to me, both Echo and Vince agreed that I should swear out the next wiretap affidavit extension request. This was a huge step for me and an absolute vote of confidence by these two hardened organized crime investigators. I was shocked but completely ready and up to the task. Echo, who explained it very simply and always to the point, said to me, "Look, you did a lot of work here, and you know the details best, so you should swear to the affidavit." Vince, who was so impressed with my abilities as an investigator, was thrilled to share the good news. I had done so much work in gaining evidentiary material that it was only natural to them that I attest to the integrity of the investigation thus far and request the eavesdropping extension, which moved the case forward.

From the extension received in that affidavit, we were about to enter the big leagues. Things would be serious from here on out. We were now targeting the head of the Gambino crime family: John Gotti "Junior." Prior to me joining the investigation, those from the DA's office who had worked the case previously demonstrated little-to-no interest in actually building a criminal case. The investigators were unmotivated, lacking both focus and basic interdisciplinary skills. To work such a case, you needed to select the team, and they needed to be committed; these folks just didn't have it.

They showed up for work simply for the perks that came with being assigned to the OCTF investigation. They had no interest to actually do the grunt work required in working a case. The lead DI investigator was eventually removed from the case for incompetence. However, while on the case, his negative impact and legacy of mediocrity, which unfortunately, is a common thread within law enforcement, was dictating the poor pace of the rest of the task force team members, and thus, the investigation. All seemed affected except me, and to his surprise, he had another thing coming to him if he thought he was going to corrupt me as well.

Prior to my arrival, an investigative strategy was developed early on and a deal brokered to conduct the investigation, sharing responsibilities between two organizations, the New York State OCTF and the Bronx DA's Office. The former supplying the technical expertise and the Intel analysts, while the latter offering up the prosecutor and investigative team members. These day-to-day investigators from the DI squad were responsible for the handling of the eavesdropping in the "plant" and surveillance. We all reported to Ercole "Echo" Gaudioso, who served as the case agent, and Vince, who served as the lead prosecutor.

As a team member, you were required to work shift work; 8 a.m. to 4 p.m., and 4 p.m. to midnight. So these were my official hours of operation where I regularly, without fanfare, reported to what was known as the "Plant." The plant was the location where the eavesdropping equipment used in the investigation was housed. Team members, myself included, would sit, stand, or both, and listen to intercepts. Intercepts were the recorded conversations by and among known and alleged Mafia associates who were intercepted by law enforcement with the full backing of a federal magistrate judge. (Remember my affidavit request.) We would or were supposed to take copious notes from these intercepts. We basically listened to these characters talk until midnight 7 days a week.

The crackerjack team sent up from the Bronx to OCTF was a complete joke. I mean, it really was comedy hour, which made for an entertaining shift at the plant, but not so much for building a case that would stick to these wise guys. There was a fellow investigator who I enjoyed known as "Vinney," who's only concern was eating his wife's home-cooked seven-course Italian meals. These homemade delicacies, at times, would get in the way of him listening to pertinent conversations.

I witnessed Echo on numerous occasions walk into the plant to share information, only to catch Vinney, headphones off, cotton napkin around his neck, silverware in hand, completely engulfed in his wife's homemade lasagna. This man, during his meals, could care less about the listening device, called a "bug" that he was required to monitor. The bug was in a paramount location, the home of Greg DePalma. He would periodically raise his head from the plate, the meal spread out across the table, notice the brass in the room, and immediately rant and rave about how wonderful the food tasted, how great a cook his wife was, and how much he loved her for it.

I can't tell you how many times I got fed up watching this *palacio*, Italian for "clown," consume his gourmet meal. I would go over to the equipment, turn up the volume on the bug, only to hear Greg DePalma in full conversation. One time, DePalma whispered to Mario Antonicelli about an issue with one of the rackets and discussed how to approach Louie Ricco. Once it was obvious to me and all present that my colleague, Cantarella, had not been paying attention, I would bark a quick order at him. "Hey, I'm going to do a 'drive-by' at the DePalma residence, so you got to listen, OK, buddy?"

He responded by closing his eyes and quickly blinking and repeating yes over and over again to me. In no time, I would run out, jump into a parked unmarked police vehicle, and within minutes, be at the DePalma residence, just in time to take down the license plate number, make, and model of the visiting mobster's vehicle, often right before he pulled away. This extra step was done simply to further "complement" what was being heard on the wiretaps. Heard was wishful thinking, at least when my boy Vinney was on shift. A physical surveillance gives further proof and leaves very little to the skeptical mind that the person heard was the same person exiting the residence. A physical description and confirmation of the vehicle as well only served as a force multiplier and played a major role in what was about to occur.

There were times when Echo would just shake his head in despair or disgust—the same thing. Other times, he would lay into Vinney, who would go into a response mode that mirrored the classic routine of Curl Howard from *The Three Stooges*. When you looked at the guy, you couldn't tell if he was actually looking at you since he had a lazy eye. He was basically a simpleton and just repeated what others said; no creativity or original ideas, and honestly was in a pickle. He was not going anywhere in law enforcement and thus, needed to be careful. Now, Rob, the supervisor for the DI squad, had a government car, the ultimate perk at the time. His only apparent concern in life was to provide just enough evidence to keep the wiretap case going indefinitely. Why would he do such a thing, I mean, work hard to keep the status quo? The answer was simple, and it pissed me off back then, and still does today. The brazen fuck enjoyed the easy assignment and wanted that car with a paid gas expense account for as long as possible. He literally would bolt out of the plant every day before his 4 p.m. shift ended, always offering up some bullshit excuse. The guy didn't care about the case and looked for every excuse to run down to the DA's office. There, he would meet with his close confidant and best buddy, the deputy chief.

Both the deputy and the chief were two buffoons. They were so filled with sloth that they had the audacity to hand me on my first day on the job a detective shield that looked like it went through the garbage disposal. I was taught early on to look your absolute best, and if I had around my neck a shield like as if my dog used it to nibble on in between meals, what would the average citizen think of me? So as soon as they handed it to me, I did what most cops do in New York; I had a duplicate, or *"dup,"* made. Then once the dup was made, I sent the original in for refurbishing. I never wore the original since it was 30 days on the beach if I lost it; basically, 30 days without pay. So I placed the badge in my home safe and wore the dup to work since technically, it was a copy, and, therefore, not accountable, nor was it valid, of course.

I grew very close to Vincent Heintz, as together, after work and often on weekends, we spent countless hours reviewing evidence and discussing case strategy and objectives. At other times, I served as his armed bodyguard as I sat at a table for hours on end at a place called the An Beal Bocht. It was here, a little cozy Irish pub that he prepared and wrote extension requests for the wiretaps. His son, only an infant at the time, sitting quietly in his car seat, right next to his dad and a pint of Guinness.

The bar was off 238th Street in Riverdale (Bronx), New York, that was in close proximity to both Vince's residence and my own. So as Vince would write his title III extensions for the case, I provided point-by-point information that came from surveillances, interviews, and from the interception/ongoing wiretaps generated out of the plant. The case which started out with an inquiry into a fellow named Lenny Minuto had, in a year's time, mushroomed into a complex multistate investigation involving senior-ranking members of the Mafia. Vince and Echo would repeatedly credit me for such progress, but I was living my dream and only wanted to do more, much more.

What I found amazing was the fact that prior to me being assigned to the OCTF case, the task force had dropped one of the wiretaps assigned to Craig DePalma's cell phone. After months of interceptions, it was incorrectly determined that the cell phone had minimal criminal value to the investigation and that DePalma was basically not really involved in the "day-to-day" criminal activities of the Gambino crime family. I began to reexamine the evidence collected during the day and evening shifts. I usually did so after my official shift ended. I would listen to the intercepted conversations and add what was missing to the transcripts.

I wrapped myself into this painstaking meticulous work where others were either too bored, too good, or did not know any better, to do so themselves. For my part, who better to do this kind of work than a kid who was raised around gangsters? I listened to these very types of men growing up as they perused the aisles of my family deli. I knew their language and understood the eccentricities of their dialect. Soon after reviewing the transcripts, I realized that a great deal of information shared on Craig DePalma's cell phone did, in fact, have tremendous investigative value. Not only was this information significant to the case, but John Gotti Junior had also called that very cell phone. Upon further review of the audiocassettes, a conversation whereby Gotti Junior personally directed Craig DePalma to meet him was also intercepted. Vinney's wife must have made homemade cannoli for dessert that night.

4

You're Nottin' but a Dirty Gutter Rat!

I was about to embark on a journey fraught with risk. The work for which I was soon to engage in was more vocation than job. It represented something beyond mere employment. It was an exertion that would totally consume me. It occupied all of my waking hours and ate into what little sleep I did get. It slowly enveloped me and helped shape all my actions, my thoughts, and relationships. It required full commitment. It demanded all of my time and energy, serving as both its source of and reason for depletion. I sacrificed a great deal but honestly would do it all over again in a New York Minute!.

I forfeited some aspects of my personal health and fun experiences common to someone my age. My marriage also fell victim. It failed, and we divorced only a few years after saying I do. I paid a price. Looking back, though, I would pay it all over again if given the choice. I absolutely loved it. I thrived off of it. I was very good at it. I was about to investigate the Gambino organized crime family. I would do this in and around Westchester County, New York, the area where I grew up dreaming of the very thing I was about to do: investigate the Mafia; both members and associates alike.

My family and friends lived in the very area where I would soon begin to probe and poke at this big tiger. The Mafia had their grasp on many facets of daily life for a New Yorker. In Westchester County, it was no different as this organized criminal syndicate maintained a very prominent role and strong presence in the construction and trash hauling business. They, however, bring a felonious element to this industry, as well as their traditional lines of business in gambling, loan sharking, and narcotics. These are but a few of their many unlawful activities.

A basic historical perspective of the Mafia and the Gambino family, in particular, is helpful to fully appreciate the actions I took against and the success I achieved in investigating organized crime. The Gambino family began its rise to the top of the Mafia food chain with the 1957 assassination of mob boss Albert Anastasia while sitting in a barber chair at the Park Sheraton Hotel in Manhattan. It was widely believed that Carlo Gambino, the underboss to Anastasia, had a hand in orchestrating the murder, or "hit," in a power move intended to take over the "family."

Prior to the 1957 assassination of Albert Anastasia, the Gambino crime family was one of the five families that were founded in New York after the Castellammarese War of 1931. The Gambino crime family occupied a minor role and place in the organized crime world during the next 25 years or so. However, during Anastasia's reign, he was both ambitious and a force with which to be reckoned. He was, in fact, the most prominent member of the criminal organization during this period. His penchant for violence and ruthlessness helped him rise up in the ranks until he became the operating head of the underworld's enforcement arm, known as Murder, Inc. Although this group was dismantled by the efforts of law enforcement in the late 1940s, Anastasia remained powerful within the organization and eventually took over the family in 1951, after allegedly murdering the family's founder, Vincent Mangano. The common theme here is the succession plan begins and ends . . . with murder.

Carlo Gambino, a visionary in some respects, partnered with Meyer Lansky to take control over the gambling interests in Cuba. All occurring, of course, pre-Bay of Pigs, Cuban missile crisis, and the political cold war and embargos that followed. Under Carlo's leadership at the head of the family, the Gambinos gained both fortune and power. In 1976, upon his own imminent death, Carlo Gambino appointed his brother-in-law Paul Castellano as boss of the family. This act pissed off a brash up-and-coming capo named John Gotti, later known as the "Teflon Don" for his ability to elude federal conviction. John Gotti, like Carlo Gambino, used violence to achieve his goals and eventually orchestrated Castellano's murder in 1985 outside the infamous Sparks Steak House in Manhattan.

The Teflon Don's own downfall eventually came about in 1992, when his underboss, Salvatore "Sammy the Bull" Gravano decided to cooperate with the FBI. Gravano's inside knowledge and secure position within the inner circle of the Mafia, coupled by his predominant desire to save his own skin, led to his becoming a cooperating witness in the case against his former friend and boss, John Gotti. His collaboration with the Department of Justice brought down Gotti, along with most of the top members of the Gambino family. With John Gotti behind bars where he eventually died of cancer, it was widely believed that Frank Cali took over as the head of the Gambino crime family.

It was 1995 and the Gambino crime family was hemorrhaging. Its organization was riddled with arrests and numerous informants among its ranks. Finally, after what seemed like an eternity on the defensive and on the end of a losing record season after season, it appeared as if now law enforcement was on firmer footing and finally making a dent in the criminal networks controlled by these men. OCTF had a case on Gregory "Greg" DePalma, of Scarsdale, New York. DePalma, a soldier in the Gambino family, had achieved fame—the worst kind.

A quarter of a century earlier, in the mid-1970s, DePalma befriended numerous A-list celebrities who often frequented his newly built nightspot, the Westchester Premiere Theatre in Tarrytown, New York. Famous people like singers Liza Minnelli and Dean Martin, and baseball legend Willie Mays, were among his new companions. In fact, DePalma and Mays regularly played golf together. However, DePalma's most renowned friend was legendary singer and American icon, Frank Sinatra. In fact, the infamous photo taken in 1976 of DePalma, Sinatra, and Gambino boss Carlo Gambino, future boss Paul Castellano, and other Gambino mobsters was taken at the Tarrytown nightspot.

As soon as the theatre opened its doors to the general public and celebrities alike, DePalma started looting its cash and other assets. In 1977, he became a "made man" in the Gambino crime family. Only a year later in June 1978, DePalma was indicted on state charges stemming from the theatre's financial collapse due to his gouging. The first trial ended in a hung jury, and later in 1979, before a second trial against him for similar charges, DePalma pleaded guilty to bankruptcy fraud. Ironic though, the one piece of evidence that helped the prosecution's case was the picture of him with Sinatra. DePalma was sentenced to 4 years in prison. In the late 1990s, DePalma was named a *caporegime* (captain) according to the FBI. He visited Gambino boss John Gotti while Gotti was incarcerated in 2001. At the time when I joined the case against the Gambinos in the mid-1990s, Greg DePalma was still a soldier in the Gambino crime family hierarchy.

During this period, Greg DePalma was promoted to "capo," a powerful and lofty position in the mob. His son, Craig, also a made man, reported to John Gotti Junior, or "Junior," as he was commonly referred. Craig was a good-looking, thin young man with an odd interest and collection of Freddy Krueger masks, while his father loved to eat Italian food. I remember early on working surveillances with Echo, where we would follow Greg to a restaurant in the Bronx called Joe Ninas, located on Westchester Avenue in the Bronx, one night, we were not there more than a few minutes, when I hear a loud crash, only to see the front of a vehicle wrapped around the steel pillar that was built to support the subway platform above.

The scene was horrific. I was the first to get to the car crash where a young man and his mother were inside the car and obviously did not survive the impact. The planned surveillance of Greg was over as Echo neared the scene, and for good reason. I can still recall the two fatally injured bodies exposed half in and half out of the vehicle with blood everywhere. Unfortunately, we did not have a chance to attempt lifesaving techniques. They were already dead upon our arrival. In New York City, approximately 40 percent of the subway system runs on surface or elevated train tracks, and the last thing you want to do is be in a head-on collision with these monster pillars.

As I stood there feeling powerless, I recall a couple shouting out my name, and as I looked up, it was two students from Fordham that I knew from my college days, now married and in the neighborhood, coincidentally walking by as I had apprehended the drunk who had stumbled out of his van and who was the cause of the accident. Both had a smile on their faces when they initially made contact with me, but that smile quickly faded. The "innocence" of life as a student in college at that moment when we looked at each other had obviously vanished. As I was handing the drunk over to the uniformed members of service that responded to the scene, it was clear our new roles had been defined, and there was no turning back.

Back at the OCTF and the ongoing intercepts, Greg DePalma would be overheard calling Joe Nina's restaurant, and before we would have to turn off the recorder, you could hear him describe, in great detail, almost salivating, the meatballs and size he preferred them to be. Greg would say, "I want them nice and big, like a football." I have never looked at a meatball since without thinking of these words and images.

No sooner than having reported to OCTF, I was assigned my very first task—and it was a big one. I was to conduct surveillance on Greg DePalma, cover his meeting, I was told, with no further information or elaboration. I was nervous, I'm sure, but tried not to show it. I must have wreaked of nervousness.

Echo approached me and in a matter-of-fact tone and a hurried manner, simply offered this guidance: "Look, don't be too aggressive and give them distance." At first, I thought this made no sense and wondered why he did not offer more specific and helpful advice. I was so wrong. No truer words, however succinct, have ever been said about the dos and don'ts of conducting a surveillance. My partner Vinney and I gathered our equipment. I was the designated driver and once ready, we jumped into a surveillance vehicle and off we went. There was no training, there was no lecture beyond the 10-second sound bite from Echo. I could not help but smile. It was actually about to happen. I would soon do surveillance on a Mafia figure.

I was driving on the local streets of Yonkers, careful to appear relaxed, cool, and not the excited rookie I really was. I noticed the target vehicle driven by John "N" beginning to speed up and slow down intermittently. What was happening? I could clearly see Greg DePalma, seated in the right front passenger seat, turning around looking back at us—at me! Now I was really confused. How could this be? I was doing my best to keep my distance while maintaining a visual on them so as not to lose them.

I was trying to make my driving and my first surveillance of them as inconspicuous as possible. It would soon become obvious that the meeting they were going to, the one I did not follow them to, was an important one, indeed. Because of this reason, these mobsters, with years of combined experience in being surveilled by police, engaged in successful countermeasures. They easily shook our two-man surveillance team that night. I quickly learned a valuable lesson . . . the first of many to come. These were serious people, and if I was to be successful, I too needed to always treat them as such. To do otherwise would be foolish and costly.

We returned to the plant, I with my tail between my legs, my pride diminished, and overcome even with a hint of sadness. Echo found my demeanor amusing. As my partner Vinney immediately began to "*cantare*," which means sing in Italian, providing every bullshit excuse, I looked up at Echo and without hesitation, said, "Yeah, we got burned." Echo could not help but smile; he knew we tried, and that was all he was looking for. "Look, don't worry; this happens, and sometimes when you think you're getting burned, in reality, you're not." I simply shook my head in disgust with myself. At the end of my shift, I went to the nearest bookstore and made sure that I grabbed every true crime book on the shelf. I read everything there was to know about the Gambino crime family.

In what seemed to be in no time at all, I was able to decipher from seemingly innocuous references and comments some valuable material that provided investigative leads. I listened to their conversations day in and day out. I learned their language, understood their jokes, and saw meaning in apparently unrelated words and topics, where others did not. At one point in the investigation, I had placed several pagers on surveillance and placed additional pen registers on locations that were of interest based on the people who were communicating. I helped Linda, the only person assigned to transcribe the intercepted communications. I found the tedious job of transcribing tapes both interesting and very helpful to adding to my overall knowledge and investigative strategy. The summer was soon coming to an end, and with less than 6 months on the job, I steadily gained confidence in my abilities, and our clandestine operation proceeded like a well-oiled machine.

One afternoon, my coworker Roger, a tall, thin, black man with a British accent, replaced me at the plant. With my shift over, Echo and I were on our way to the local bar in White Plains. The plant was closed from midnight to 0800 hours, so Roger would cover the 4 p.m. to midnight shift. Earlier that day, I had intercepted an unknown meeting off of Craig DePalma's cell phone. This was the same cell phone that was once tapped but soon after being intercepted, it was deemed useless and promptly shut down. I continued the practice of listening to audiotapes and follow the transcripts after my regular shifts were over. After listening to several dozen cassette recordings, I noticed that John Gotti Junior, or someone that sounded a lot like him, was calling Craig from a place called JAG Construction. Later in the investigation, OCTF was able to verify the voice intercepted on the previous affidavit for the cell phone was, in fact, Junior's.

Now that I was fully able to articulate to both my supervisors and the

United States Attorney's Office that Junior was calling Craig, the cell phone's significance to the case grew exponentially. The cryptic conversations between Junior and Craig, who were obviously attempting to evade potential law enforcement, now demanded even closer attention and scrutiny. The fact that both Junior and Craig were half Jewish and half Italian was an ironic fact that always intrigued me. Given their nonauthentic Italian bloodline, these two men could have never been "made" in the Mafia, if not for their respective fathers.

The son of "the" John Gotti, or for that matter, "the" Greg DePalma, were forgiven an otherwise incontestable tenant of Mafia tradition. Anyway, I emphasized to Roger the importance of the call that was made earlier and to let both Echo and I know of any follow-up call that may follow. Echo said "Let's go," and off we went to our night of doo-wop music, dinner, followed up by maybe chasing women. On our walk from OCTF to the bar, Echo explained to me that sometimes all that is needed is taking an extra step or two, putting in the extra effort at work, and an urgent sense of curiosity to give cases the acceleration needed so progress can begin.

He continued offering me words of encouragement, mixed with a bit of venting over his frustration with the lack of effort put forth by some members of the team. Before Echo could say another word and complete his rant, he was interrupted by a long-forgotten beeping sound put forth by the Motorola pager, a staple in the 1990s. The notification on his pager was music to our ears. It was the plant. I immediately dug into my pocket and retrieved loose change and found the nearest pay phone. Roger, manning the plant, told me that Craig had just been summoned and he needs to meet "him" at Liberty Avenue in Queens.

I repeated the message relayed to me in almost real time as I was hearing it. Echo and I simply looked at each other and did not utter a single word. We headed back to OCTF, grabbed a work car, and hightailed it to Queens, New York. Under normal traffic conditions, the drive time should take about 45 minutes to cover the 32-mile distance. This was not normal in any way. It was the start of rush hour, the 5 p.m. gridlock in full swing. Our saving grace was the fact that we were headed against the heavy flow of traffic. The ride remained a bit of a blur for me, as I don't think we spoke too much. Both of us were quiet, certainly thinking of the possibilities that could unfold. I pushed that government vehicle to its limits and showed complete disregard for safety, driving over 100 mph down the Hutchinson River Parkway and over the Whitestone Bridge toward Queens.

I was determined to pass Craig, get ahead of him, and arrive on set before he did. The highway, with all its curves and nuances, was all seemingly distorted by the blur of me passing every car in my wake. The mixture of sounds and colors of these vehicles was almost hypnotic. We were running hot and silent. What I do recall was Echo, strapped into his seat, clutching the passenger door with his right hand while his left held the glove compartment. He was bracing himself for the inevitable impact and kept saying that he didn't know who was more dangerous—the Gambinos or my driving!

I remember pulling off the Van Wyck Expressway at Liberty Avenue and circling back around, when Echo spotted Craig DePalma's car, a silver Chevy Blazer. I positioned my car behind Craig's at a safe but effective distance. I was not going to get burned on this one, not again. The Blazer then pulled alongside and linked up with another vehicle, a black Oldsmobile. Echo and I shared a pair of binoculars and could see Craig talking to two men.

As the cars pulled away, we could not believe it. There was John Gotti

Junior seated on the passenger side of the Oldsmobile. We made the vital connection. The link between DePalma and the Gambino crime boss was established. It was this connection that enabled us to obtain judicial approval for and placement of wiretaps on Gotti's phones and bug his offices. What a productive night—a cause for celebration indeed.

After about 2 hours or so, Echo determined it was best to depart the set. However, the excitement was not yet over. Shortly after driving away, while on Sutphin Boulevard, we noticed *we* were being followed. Our "tail" was a dark Suburban with three men inside. Echo quickly jotted the license plate down, and we eventually discovered the car was registered to Carmine Agnello's junkyard business. Agnello, was Gotti Junior's brother-in-law and also a suspected member of the Gambino crime family.

They positioned themselves along my right front bumper at a red light, rolled down the windows, and one of the men asked, "How's it going?" Their hands were hidden, and their eyes were trained on us. I thought at that moment, I fully expected to see a shotgun being pulled out from below the car window, when I saw Echo reach into the glove compartment, only hours ago that he clutched with his life, and pulled out a police parking credential. Echo flashed it and mumbled something to the effect of "We're good guys, just working." The guy in the passenger seat looked at us and mumbled something as they quickly drove away.

Despite, or partly because of, the momentary crisis faced when confronted by these three goons, both Echo and I were on a natural high. We were absolutely euphoric. Somehow, we arrived in time. This was amazing as Craig had at least a good 10- to 15-minute lead on us. OCTF had actually intercepted a telephone call from Gotti

Junior summoning Craig. The meeting took place with Junior and Craig DePalma in what appeared to be an abandoned warehouse, and we were there to witness and record every incriminating moment of it. We were now getting closer to moving up the food chain of the Gambino hierarchy.

I became so obsessed with listening to every intercepted word and pondering over the written transcripts, that as I sat at the plant, before, during, and after my shifts, I could easily identify, by name, every voice that was transmitted over our sanctioned listening devices. My knowledge of the players, both the starters and those who sat on the bench, so to speak, became a permanent part of my memory. I could easily recall and discuss their specific roles in the family business, as well as other tidbits of useless information that one acquired only after spending countess hours listening to every word uttered from their mouths, and, boy, did these guys like to talk.

One day, before the start of my shift at the plant, we executed a search warrant at Greg DePalma's residence, where he lived with his mob son, Craig. Now, as I sat listening to telephone conversations, I hoped to hear some information I could readily associate with their criminal activity. A telltale sign that whenever two known members of the crime family were about discuss something of note, the volume on the TV would suddenly increase. If the volume went up, people were going to talk business.

Sometimes, we would synchronize our search warrants at various mob locations so as to increase our chances of gleaming valuable information from the telephone conversations that would ensue after law enforcement left the premises. This technique unfolded over time after some trial and error and was known as "tickling" the bug.

One time, in between minimizations, I heard Greg DePalma, in a fit of rage, yelling at what appears to be his wife. We were curious as to the cause of his anger and endless use of profanity. We listened to the rant for the legally permissible amount of time, and then minimized the call only to resume after the required pause. On this occasion, after the earlier execution of a search warrant at his home, Greg was furious because the OCTF investigators had found and seized his stash of marijuana, used for his personal enjoyment.

Something beautiful happened in between the barrage of insults directed toward his wife and "those fucking scumbag cops." There was a slight pause and in a low whisper, DePalma expressed his pleasure and relief that the money hidden in the rafters was never uncovered during the search. Greg, I would soon find out, had an uncontrollable mouth. It was as if he was compelled to elaborate and provide mundane details on every topic, albeit "business" or what he had for lunch.

A few days later, after obtaining the required legal approvals, we went back to his home and recovered the money, over $250,000, only to confuse and disorient him even more. After this discovery, just like before, I could hear Greg in the midst of yet another verbal tirade filled with fury and insults. This one, however, was solely directed toward his wife. The argument this time centered on his use of recreational drugs. In between the minimization, I heard Greg speak the following slur: "You're a rat . . . a dirty gutter rat, you're nottin' but a dirty gutter rat." It was as sad as it was comical. As soon as we realized that he was saying this to his wife of over 30 years, Terry, we once again minimized the call.

The case was now moving along rather nicely. Most of the "dead wood" on the team had been removed with the remaining having begun to take the assignment seriously. As I learned more about our targets and became more experienced, I was allowed more investigative flexibility and responsibilities. Echo and Vince were pleased with my performance. I was satisfying my lifelong dream. Things were good. Once again, the opportunity presented itself for me to push the investigative envelope. I could not contain myself during these moments. Filled with overconfidence and a sense of purpose, I directed my efforts toward a new avenue of approach, not previously undertaken at OCTF.

I requested a court order to clone the younger DePalma, Craig's, pager. For those of you who are unaware of what a pager is, it is basically an electronic device that either receives a basic message, typically a phone number, and/or later devices one could receive and send written messages. Thus, I would receive notification in real time whenever he received a page. This was a fantastic tool, however, one which took me some time to figure out how to best use it to our advantage. As I was trying to understand the strange beeps, both in sequence and digits that Craig received on his pager, I noticed a pattern. Over the course of several weeks, I noticed the receipt of a page sent only on Wednesdays. The phone toll records also confirmed a pattern of numbers, in no discernable sequence, only sent on Wednesday afternoons. An example of this occurrence was a page that had the following numbers: 101900 or 101930.

It was a Wednesday. While reading yet another true crime book on the Gambino family during my shift at the plant, a breakthrough occurred. I read a line on a page that described the Bergin Hunt and Fish Club. There it was, the physical address of this storied hangout made famous by the legendary mob boss John J. Gotti Sr., who was also known as the "Dapper Don." It was located at 98-04 101st Avenue in Ozone Park. The Bergin Hunt and Fish Club, a former Gambino crime family mob hangout and headquarters, was well known. Holy shit, could it be possible that Craig was being summoned to 101st Street and the numbers that followed on the pager was the time to report? It made sense, right? 101900—could it actually mean to meet at the location, at 9 p.m.? It was a brilliant maneuver on their part. The obvious was hidden in plain sight.

Despite the numerous surveillances conducted on the location by untold police agencies, and regardless of the fact that the club was a confirmed Mafia joint, it remained the place where mob boss John Gotti Junior held court. Again, in these types of investigations, sometimes the obvious was not so obvious at first glance. I ran my theory by both Echo and Vince, who were amazed and in agreement that we should initiate a surveillance the next time a similar page was sent. Like clockwork, the following week, Wednesday, to be exact, the page was sent with the code: 101900. Although nothing but a hunch, I believed a 9 p.m. meeting was being signaled. Of course, there was no response from Craig. They were too seasoned to tip off anyone who may be monitoring their communications.

With our teams chosen, strategy set, and ops briefings completed, we set off on our surveillance of the infamous Bergin Hunt and Fish Club. Again, I could not contain my excitement and inner sense of pride. It was almost surreal. Here I was with my partner Roger about to hit the streets. What brought me back to reality, to the dangers involved in pursuing these men, was the simple fact of the car I was in. A white Ford Pinto. This car was the definition of noticeable. How ridiculous, but there was no time to object and no one would have listened. Things were moving fast with no time to debate.

The OCTF team was in place, all strategically positioned to cover every possible direction in and out of the club. There was much activity in the area, with cars moving up and down the street and neighbor-hood people loitering on the sidewalks. It was around 8:30 p.m., approximately 30 minutes before the 9:00 p.m. meeting. I saw two hulking men step out of the club, one of them carrying a baseball bat. They began to canvass the immediate area and challenge everyone seated in a vehicle. One by one, the surveillance vehicles are identi-fied and rather than get into a potential altercation, my OCTF partners left the surveillance.

They chose to restage away from the Bergin, break the surveillance, and fight another day. As these two "*chooches*" approach my vehicle, I looked at Roger seated in the passenger seat. He understandably looked frightened but before either of us could speak and muster a plan, I grabbed him by his head and firmly placed it in the direction of my lap. "What the fuck are you—" he said, but I told him to shut up and keep his head down. From a distance, it looked like I was getting a blowjob. I leaned back in my chair and pretended to be enjoying myself, all the while keeping a close eye on the two men slowly ap-proaching our Pinto, with one hand on my partner's head and the other on my .38 snub-nosed revolver. The men came within 20 feet or so, looked at each other, looked back at me with a faux look of joy, turned, and walked away.

That night, Roger and I collected some great evidence as we wit-nessed some key players showing up at the club to pay homage to John Gotti Junior. The path now clearly defined—we were moving up the organized crime food chain. The hunt was underway, and they had no idea what was about to happen. Like a dog on a hunt, I too felt unstoppable and knew it was only a matter of time when I would capture my prey. However, in the short term, I had a lot of explaining and ball busting to do with my friend Roger.

5

First Impressions by Design . . .

As my time at OCTF came to a conclusion, my last great act and contribution was swearing to the December 1995 state affidavit. The significance of this investigative technique and judicial act was groundbreaking to the overall direction and impact of the investigation thus far. This affidavit, sanctioned by U.S. Magistrate Judge Sondra Miller, Appellate Division, authorized the interception team to extend the scope and number of targets to be surveilled by wiretap.

Why was this so important? This affidavit enabled us to methodically move up the criminal food chain and set our sights on the head of the Gambino crime family—John Gotti Junior, himself. This was truly an unbelievable accomplishment, and I was extremely proud. I felt good that the investigation into the Gambinos was moving along with a renewed focus on the "boss" . . . Junior. I found myself, once again, on a new but somewhat familiar path, moving onto another challenge, another job, and another step in achieving my lifelong dream of becoming a federal agent.

The year was 1996 and after the recruitment, application, and training process came to a successful end, finally, I was ready to begin my life as special agent with the United States Secret Service. It seemed at the time to be a good fit, and since it was the first federal law enforcement agency offering me a job, as the saying goes, "a bird in the hand is worth two in the bush." I never looked back.

At the Secret Service, the vetting process was absolutely "no joke". So when it came to the polygraph phase, which for me was a grueling 3-hour process, the person who administered the exam was an agent who looked like the real Jason Bourne. His name was Rich Staropoli. To this day I joke about his presence and of course his professionalism during my polygraph experience. Let me say this, Rich is a very dear friend who is extremely successful in the private sector and someone who at a moment's notice you can absolutely count on...

After 6 months between two training academies, the Federal Law Enforcement Training Academy in Glynco, Georgia, and the United States Secret Service Academy in Laurel, Maryland, I was ready. Ready to start my career, but even more so to get back to New York City and to the real world. I often felt inhibited, constrained, and downright claustrophobic in classroom settings. Now, I was a newly commissioned, brand-spanking-new special agent. The day I swore an oath to defend the American public and the United States Constitution as a Secret Service agent was, and remains, one of the proudest moments of my life.

I reported to 7 World Trade Center, the home of the respected New York Field Office (NYFO). All new Secret Service agents in the New York Field Office (NYFO), regardless of professional background and experience (some were police, detectives, and lawyers in previous careers), were assigned to the check forgery squad. This was a training squad, so to speak, whereby agents were given what seemed like countless forged Treasury check cases to investigate.

These investigations involved the new agent, many of whom were prior law enforcement, to learn the basic tools of investigations. All check cases, the majority of which were forged to reflect either a higher amount than the original dollar amount of the check (altered check case), a forged payee signature, and often a false claim (theft of check) made by the original payee in hopes to double down on his/her benefit check which were either monthly Social Security income and/or disability checks or tax refunds.

The check squad was the place and a way for the office to indoctrinate the new recruits and teach them how to do things the New York way. This, by no means, implied breaking the law or violating people's rights. However, New York City is a far different animal than, say, a small town in the Midwest, and a brand-new Secret Service agent assigned to the NYFO had better learn how to tame this animal if he wanted to be successful and gain the respect of his peers.

One afternoon, my friend and I, another "check agent" as we were affectionately called, went out to Brooklyn to "investigate" a check case which, in reality, meant to obtain as much information as possible to close the case out before we were to begin our 3-week travel rotations in support of President Clinton's 1996 reelection campaign. As I think about it, check agent was often used to advertise to the more seasoned workforce that we were still green and rough around the edges.

So we set out for what should be a quick 15-minute drive to Brooklyn, just over the Brooklyn Bridge, but due to the traffic downtown, it takes us an hour and a half. We drive to our destination in an old beat-up Crown Victoria ("Crown Vic" as it is known among law enforcement) that wreaks like a police car. Oh, I must also mention that because of the new dress code enforced upon us by our new supervisor (assistant to the special agent, or ATSAIC, or better yet, AT, as they were called), my partner and I had to wear business suits. Yes, as ridiculous as it sounds, it was far worse in reality.

This supervisor did not like his guys wearing dress-down clothes so as to blend somewhat in the neighborhoods where we spent most of our time investigating fraud cases. He felt we needed to "look the part." He obviously had not worked a criminal case ever, and he certainly had no idea of the New York City animal I explained earlier. Normally, what we would do is keep a pair of jeans, sneakers, and a T-shirt in our G rides and change in the World Trade Center parking garage, the same place which had been bombed in the 1993 attack. Having to sneak and change clothes in the garage felt like we were some teenage schoolgirls sneaking out of their homes to go to a house party,

So we arrive at the target residence located in the projects. My partner is driving and expressed his reluctance to park the obviously looking police car right in front of the building where our subject lived. I, for my part, insisted he park the car as close to the front door as possible because I was hot enough in my suit and was already sweaty from the long car ride with no AC. My friend was concerned about having the vehicle towed, or worse yet, vandalized by the adult males who were loitering in and around the area. I told him I could give a rat's ass if they set the car on fire; in fact, it would be a blessing in disguise.

He parked the car, and as we got out, I saw a man in his early 30s standing against a wall. This guy seemed down on his luck, so I called him over. He looked at me and at first refused to do so as he knows I'm the police. I convinced him to walk over and introduced myself. I asked him if he knew me. He said he thinks so but was not sure. At this point, the group of guys I mentioned have taken notice of me talking to this guy and are staring me and my friend down. I told the guy, "Listen, all is good, and no worries. See that car?" He said, "Yeah, I see it . . ." "OK, that car belongs to my friend here. He loves that car; lost his virginity in that car." The guy laughed. I told him, "Do me a favor. I have a job for you . . . You need a job?" "Yeah, sure," he grunted. "OK, OK, if I give you some money, you watch my friend's car, make sure your boys don't fuck with it." "Yeah, I can do that," he said, now really interested in what I have to say.

I told my partner to give me some money; He looked at me as if to say, "I don't want to give him my money." I didn't give him a choice. I told him, "You cheap fuck, pay my guy here so he can watch the car or you do the paperwork and explain to our prick AT why you went to Brooklyn with a piece-of-shit Crown Vic and returned with only a steering wheel." My friend reached in his wallet and pulled out a $10 bill. I gave him a cross look and feigned disgust. "C'mon, you are a big-time federal agent. Give my boy $20 and stop the nonsense. Now let's go and get this shit over with," I said as I promised the guy if he did a good job, I'd have another twenty spot for him.

We entered the building and stand out like a sore thumb based on our goofy attire and the fact that, I guess, we looked like agents. We knocked on the door; can't remember what floor the lady lived on. "Who's there?" we heard. "The police," I said in a loud voice. "I ain't call no police," she screamed. I replied back, "You want your check refund or not?" She opened the door and gave us both a big smile. The lady was very overweight and was wearing, I guess you would call it a housedress, which did a poor job of covering her up. Let's just say we thought we had seen enough of her; however, as the interview unfolded, we were about to see a hell of lot more . . .

We were led into her kitchen and seated at a round table. The apartment, quite frankly, was disgusting. It smelled like cockroaches, and it was no surprise that the place was infested with them. We asked her if she was alone, other than the young kids we saw in the living room. She advised she was alone, and we conducted, with her consent, a quick safety check of the premises to ensure there were no hidden dangers. So we sat at the table, and we asked her to explain what happened with her refund check. I recall she was originally from Jamaica, and her accent was strong. My partner and I listened attentively as she attempted to explain how her check must have been stolen from the broken mailbox in the building's lobby. This process was changed years ago whereby Treasury checks are directly deposited now into the payees' account to avoid the fraud, which we worked so diligently years ago to uncover.

The lady explained a very creative and elaborate story how she thinks she knows the group of men who stole her check when my friend, who was the case agent, continued to employ all the techniques we learned in Secret Service school as he nodded his head, listened attentively, and appeared nonjudgmental. He and I agreed with her, and I told her we have been working hard on such a crime syndicate in the area. This is, of course, all bullshit—both my story and definitely her story as well. So neither my buddy nor I are buying what she is selling, so we employ the hardnosed tactic right away, asking for her, as a matter of protocol, to sign her name on government-issued handwriting sample cards.

These cards resembled a long-sized rectangular-shaped index card, except they were not white but almost a yellowish-brown color. We had her sign her name on about 100 cards that day. The first 20 or so, it was apparent she was trying her hardest to conceal her actual signature from which we would compare to the back of the returned "stolen" check. We told her we would use these samples to convince our boss, the guy who made us wear these suits to her house, that she was not guilty. We told her that we believed she was, in fact, a good and honest woman who would NEVER commit fraud against the United States government and file a false claim, would she? "No, mon," she kept saying.

So back to the incessant handwriting samples we were obtaining from her. She kept telling us that her hand hurt and asked if she could she stop . . . "No, just a few more to go. You know government paperwork and all . . ." It became clear that after about 15 minutes of the tiring monotony of writing your name over and over and over, her best efforts and attempts to hide her actual signature failed. They failed in a big-time way!

We were by no means handwriting experts, but it only took a person with half a brain to instantly recognize and make a positive comparison between handwriting samples #50 through #100 to the back of the supposedly "stolen" T check. At this point, we had her; we broke her. We told her that she would be charged to the fullest extent of federal law for committing such a horrible crime, when, in fact, the United States Attorney's Office would never have even accepted the case for criminal prosecution due to the low-dollar amount of the actual check. But what the hell! She did not need to know that. Hell, we had a case to close and city traffic to navigate on our way back to Lower Manhattan to write this "dog" up. We would call cases that were a waste of time "dogs," and in those early days of my career, it seemed I had an entire kennel to feed.

Now this woman was crying hysterically, yelling, and appeared to be close to either fainting or having a heart attack. Like I said, she was a BIG woman, and neither my partner nor I wanted to be faced with the dilemma of having to initiate mouth-to-mouth rescue techniques on her should she drop on the kitchen floor.

Realizing that we may have pushed too far with the empty threats of facing hard time in a federal prison, all bullshit, of course, we offered her an out. Just give us a good reason, you know, so we can tell our boss why you did this . . . perhaps you were mistaken and confused when you signed the claim of a stolen check. "Yeah, you right, mon," she said. "You know I was in a car accident, had me an operation and high blood pressure . . . You know me were confused on the month, you know . . . Maybe I did get that check . . . Now me think about it." "Yes, that's what happened," I told her. "Now, what kind of operation did you have?" my partner asked. He could not just leave it at her admission. He had to know what damn type of procedure she had . . . You know me, go under the knife, look at me scar. "Where and what operation?" he asked again.

I have an uneasy feeling now because she obviously had no operation and is trying hard to back the line of BS she just gave. "Look at me scar, mister," she said as she grabbed her left breast and whipped out the biggest, flattest, nastiest looking thing I have ever seen. It was so big that it almost knocked over the handwriting samples laid out across the table. I mean, the roaches even scattered at the sight of it. She insisted there was a scar under her tit caused by this made-up car accident she was involved in, which affected her memory, thus, causing her confusion and memory loss as to having, indeed, received, signed for, and cashed the subject check. My friend looked the other way as if chivalry were, in fact, still alive. He was clearly embarrassed, mortified, or both.

I started laughing my ass off and asked her to pull it out again so I . . . I mean, we, could get a better look in case we had to testify in court. I did this just to bust my friend's balls. She whipped it out as my friend gathered all the paperwork and saw himself to the door, thanking her for her time and honesty.

We got on the elevator, left the building, and headed to our car which was not only in the same place, but it was untouched by the locals, and guess who was standing watch by the right front bumper . . . my man from when we first arrived. "Look here, guys," he said, "I wiped it down for you; it's clean . . ." He smiled at us. I told him he is the man as I tell my partner to hurry up and open the door. The guy was standing around next to me as my partner fiddle fucked for the keys. I said, "What's taking so long? Open the damn door." He said to me, "Nino . . . Aren't you going to give him more money?" This guy, I loved him like a brother, but c'mon, are you serious? I say to him . . . "What's wrong with you? You got money like that to burn? I sure don't . . . Now let's get the fuck outta here. I want to change outta my suit!"

As a young man, I was polite but shy. In my early teens, I would be embarrassed to serve customers or would have my mom or dad complete an order if someone would compliment me as I was serving them. Yet, despite this shyness, I was always a mischievous kid, and due to the long hours I was forced to work at the deli, I had no recourse but to use it as my playground. But as I got older, my naughty side began to diminish and in its place, a more confident and responsible personality soon developed. Almost overnight, I began to catch the eye of female customers and would quite often be the recipient of their admiring comments.

I took on more of the hard work around the store, frequently and singlehandedly lifting the heavy shipment of produce and merchandise in an effort to help ease the burden on my aging father and to also get stronger. As my muscles began to take shape and grow, so did my confidence. I became fascinated with looking at myself and would go to the bathroom in the back storeroom to sneak a peek at my muscles or straighten out my always perfectly combed hair. If, however, I spent more than a minute in the bathroom admiring myself, my grandmother would track me down and bang on the door while yelling at me in Italian to stop whatever I "was doing" and get out to serve the waiting customers.

I had slowly transformed from a pudgy shy kid into a confident teenager. I treated the deli counter as my stage and the customers as my audience. I began to really enjoy interacting with them, listening to their stories, telling jokes, and always on the lookout for girls. I learned a great deal about people in that store. Most importantly, I became really comfortable in my ability to relate to people and empathize with their struggles.

I rarely had time off between school and work, but on the rare occasion I did have free time, I managed to get into trouble. One time, when I was about 13 years old, I managed to get a hold of my father's .38-caliber snubbed-nose revolver, without his knowledge, of course, and went to the local pizzeria to buy a "slice," as we called it in New York. I noticed some "wannabe tough guys" maybe just a few years older than I, causing a bit of a scene in the pizza shop. I took matters into my own hands, part cop, part gangster—and completely stupid—I showed them the weapon, concealed in my waistband, and told them to get the "fuck out" of my shop. I often got into trouble for fighting and once threatened a kid that I would shove his head inside the pizza oven. However, with the passing of time and a continuous string of beatings from my father, I slowly began to mature and get onto the right path.

During my evolution from a part-time juvenile delinquent to a young adult focused on becoming a public servant, I discovered something amazing. Women liked me, and I became rather adept at exploiting this mutual attraction. Female customers who regularly shopped at the deli would often bring their daughters, and even their granddaughters, with them. It became obvious, their intention was only to introduce me to them. As my younger brother Anthony got older, he too was included in this equation, but he never quite seemed to catch on. I, however, had no problem with this kind of math, and unlike my performance at school, this was a subject in which I quickly adapted and excelled.

I took advantage of this newfound opportunity and found it rather addictive. The more I worked the counter and served the customers, the more opportunity I had to flirt with the women, and occasionally find myself in the parking lot for what we called back then, a "hookup." It was so much fun, and as a 17-, 18-, and even a 19-year-old with my hormones raging and father demanding I work all the time, it was the only way I could release a little tension. I was working the counter where I learned to listen to people and developed my ability to be quick with my tongue. Whenever I was faced with a challenging situation or confronted by a dissatisfied customer, I learned how to diffuse the tension. I learned how to effectively deal with people of all types. These interpersonal skills helped me years later in my law enforcement career.

I was a good kid deep down, who simply needed some parental attention. I know my parents loved me; they were just unsure or unwilling to outwardly express it. Admittedly, I was a difficult child who needed to be challenged and allowed to pursue my dreams. My childhood was filled with bittersweet memories and experiences. Although not an uncommon sentiment, I often felt that some of my experiences were unique and absolutely contributed to my successes . . . and shortcomings in life.

I never drank, I never smoked, and I never did drugs. This lack of abuse confused many, and it sort of kept people off guard and ever guessing as to what exactly motivated me. Many people assumed I must have "been on something" or was putting on an act when I would walk up to any girl, or woman, for that matter, and ask her out. Or how I would challenge anyone in the neighborhood, tough guy or not. My courage was internal, fueled by years of pent-up energy stored inside me.

I was always full of energy, again a source of puzzlement, and even scorn, by some around me. The fact that I was like this and always had a smile on my face made people nervous and uncomfortable. They could never quite figure me out. It was not unusual for me to start work with Dad at 4 a.m., where we would head to the Hunts Point Market in the Bronx to buy produce, work a 13-hour day, and after finishing up, changing into my shorts and T-shirt and run home from Mount Vernon to Eastchester, New York. Afterward, I would get showered and dressed to go out clubbing. I never needed to be on drugs, as some often assumed. My energy was natural, and my adrenalin homemade.

I recall the time when having completed my obligatory 14-week training at the Federal Law Enforcement Training Center, I was awaiting my start date to begin the Secret Special Agent Training Course in Beltsville, Maryland. I was at the Secret Service office at 7 World Trade Center working on some type of administrative requirement before beginning my real training at the Secret Service Academy. I was dressed in black jeans, shirt, boots, and a leather MC jacket, holding a black motorcycle helmet, making copies.

My soon-to-be buddy Michael was in his cubicle in the New York Field Office (NYFO, as it was commonly called) check squad one afternoon typing reports using the old floppy disk program called WordPerfect. Although still a new agent himself, he had been in the office for a few months and was slowly getting accustomed to the workflow, expectations, and unspoken rules of conduct expected of all Secret Service agents in New York. It was a typical day in the squad with the normal ebb and flow of people walking around, telephones ringing, and the occasional sound of laughter coming from various offices or from groups of agents who would always seem to gather around the desk of someone who was trying to get his work done. Above the normal noise level, Michael heard something unusual, the continuous sound of the copy machine cranking out page after page. He looked out from his cubicle and saw me working the machine.

I stood out Big Time. I totally did not look or dress the part of a Secret Service agent, at least, not one that he had seen in the field office, or anywhere, for that matter. I was wearing a tight-fitting pair of black jeans, some type of T-shirt, can't remember the color, although it was most likely black as well, a black leather coat, the one you see bikers wearing, with what looked like silver buttons or spikes on the shoulders. I wore these biker boots with the square toe you see mostly bikers wear. Michael was confused, and he thought maybe I was there to fix the copy machine or something. I recall him explaining how he was intrigued and continued to watch me. He actually got up from his chair and, feigning some excuse, walked around and retrieved some form from a file cabinet near where I was standing, the guy in black who was making copy after copy.

He noticed in plain view, next to me on an empty desk, and wondered how he missed it—a black motorcycle helmet with tinted visor. Thinking to himself, he was sure all that walked around the check squad that day, dressed in the standard generic kakis and Polo shirts, wondered who this Italian-looking guy was dressed like he was going to a Brooklyn nightclub or something and what he was doing here with us. So Michael had to do it . . . He walked over and said hello, and then he experienced it with his own ears the words he would grow accustomed to hearing over the years, said to countless people, agents, prosecutors, general public, criminals, and more . . . *"Hi, hi, there, how are you? . . . I'm Nino . . . Nino Perrotta."*

Michael grew to understand me, and we remain dear friends to this day. Although we are both much older now, and hopefully, wiser, I hope to, one day, be able to tell his children who their father was back in the day. He was a totally loyal person who pulled no punches and was always there for everyone. Michael was an outstanding agent who cared about the product he produced, but more importantly, cared about people.

We had many similarities in that we were both basically loners and would often go on the prowl together, although his taste or standard in women differed drastically from my own. In this regard, we were complete opposites. It wouldn't be a surprise to see Michael late at night in a club somewhere in the barrios of Queens or the Bronx and working very hard to connect, so to speak, with a woman. He would laugh with a big smile whenever he saw me looking at him with complete disgust as he failed to meet my very high standards. He would often say, "What do you want from me? My track record is not as good as yours." But he was there for me, as I was there for him.

There are a few others whom I met and became friends with who met this level of respect. People who are still on the job like Jim M., Chris F. and those that have retired like Bobby Weaver, Michael Vaiani and Jack Shaughnessy. These were, and remain, truly dedicated public servants who represent the best our country has to offer and embody the definition of patriots. There were many other good men and women who believed in the job and worked hard. Well, let's just say *most* worked hard, while others played politics. In the end, though, isn't that the case everywhere? I was different, sometimes to my own detriment, but I cared only about one thing and that was becoming a mob buster with one caveat. This time, as special agent of the Secret Service. I liked the sound of it.

By the time I completed the U.S. Army training, the Rockland Police academy, and the Secret Service training, most of all of my unfocused and often-misdirected energy was now channeled toward catching criminals. I absolutely loved the hunt and reveled in unraveling the unknown pieces that are part of any investigation. This activity, both mentally and physically demanding, kept me focused and on point. Prior to discovering my passion, absolutely nothing could keep me on point. Once I finally discovered my true passion, the pursuit of bad guys became what was a new chapter in my life.

During this time of intense investigative activity and in the years immediately following, I, regrettably, was neither a good boyfriend nor a good husband. I was typically most comfortable and fulfilled when on a mission. I avoided all responsibility and commitment absent my passion for investigations. Early on, it was Echo who looked at me with a surprised look on his face and said that I had a gift. At first, I didn't understand what he meant, then with time and further explanation, I realized his point. It was somewhat easy for me to almost verbalize prediction on what would happen in a particular setting or case, then to see it play out as I predicted. I was becoming a damn good investigator. Hunches would turn into solid investigative leads. I loved receiving Echo's compliments, and in some ways, he was a father figure to me and also someone I greatly admired. He was a serious lawman. He had over 30 years of consequential law enforcement experience.

I also realized that in many ways I too was very much like Echo. He was a bit of a loner who enjoyed good food, good music, and women. Today, as I reflect on it, I would have never been satisfied in the Secret Service if I had not investigated the Mafia and worked on putting the mobsters in jail. So I began to do what I felt most comfortable doing—diving deep into my case file, taking the necessary steps to make cases, all the while oblivious of the looks and negative talk that surrounded me. Soon, very soon, the office and the agency would learn of my abilities and my commitment to the job and to the victims of crime. But for now, it was best for me to maintain a low profile, do my job, and continue to be the person I was, no matter how the popular culture reacted . . . or rejected me for it.

6

When Working Cases, You Are Bound to Meet a Few "Mamelukes"

It was January of 1997, I had been on the job for a year and had, at this time, already established myself as a tenacious investigator in spite of, and due to, my colorful personality. A new Assistant to the Special Agent in Charge (ATSAIC) was now assigned to the Treasury check squad, my squad at 7 World Trade Center. My new boss had a studious look, probably due to the rimless metal glasses he wore, and carried himself around the office in an aloof and somewhat distracted manner. He never seemed engaged, whether by design or intention. He was, without question, a bit odd, and was not favored by his subordinates.

For some reason, we bonded. He was extremely good to me despite his inability to lead us young agents or provide sound guidance toward anything investigative. He was, in my opinion, and I was in the minority, a huge improvement over my previous boss. His predecessor, who in my neighborhood of Mt. Vernon, would be known as **"mameluke."** It is a derogatory term in Italian, which equates to calling someone a "simpleton" . . . The village idiot. This guy was very outgoing and personable. His gregarious personality made him a crowd favorite . . . but not with me. He smiled whenever he saw me, but I knew he had already made up his mind on who and what I was. He was Irish, and I was Italian. We were both passionate individuals and hotheaded, heated by nature. We never quite got along.

Now it was a Friday afternoon, a typical cold winter afternoon in downtown New York City. Almost everyone in the office was gone. In the federal government, especially in those days, Fridays were called "Federal Friday," which signified an early departure time and a head start on the weekend. Usually those not assigned to late-night surveillance or protection would slowly begin to leave the building around 1:00 p.m. Most who had family would head home in an effort to beat the rush-hour traffic. Others would grab a quick beer at the many bars within walking distance along the Wall Street area of downtown Manhattan.

For Secret Service agents, there was always the ever-present third option that loomed over us like a black cloud: the reporting to a protective assignment. That meant you were already in a suit geared up at the office for an in-town assignment or heading to an airport to board a flight to some part of the country to assume your role as a part of a Secret Service protective security detail. The sporadic and unpredictable nature of this aspect of an agent's job was not easy on the personal life. It worked against the fabric of a typical federal agent's work environment. In the Secret Service, the word *typical* is not part of the vocabulary. It did not define who we were, nor what we did every day.

The Secret Service was always a way of life, a proud and honorable way to serve our country. At times, more often than not, it seemed all-encompassing; the requirements consumed your every moment and left little free time. Yet despite this, we all shared a certain esprit de corps, a brotherhood, not present in most government jobs. I was, and remain proud of being, a part of the Secret Service. There were those to whom the burdens of the job were too cumbersome and would leave, either to other government jobs or to the private sector. These men and women too played their part and served toward a greater purpose. The potential for burnout was always a factor among the workforce, and in many ways, has only increased over the years given the post-911 landscape in which law enforcement must operate.

My phone at my desk rang, and it was a fellow female agent on the tenth floor looking to punt a potential case that had been recently assigned to the bank fraud squad. She started by claiming she was too busy to handle the complaint herself. This agent had been assigned to the bank fraud squad directly right out of the academy, a coveted position, while the "less" fortunate, like myself, needed to prove to everyone that I was "capable" and thus, assigned as a grunt in the Treasury check squad. It amazed and annoyed me back then as a young man, just at the cusp of a 2-decade career in law enforcement, how senior management handled this situation.

I will tell you that part of the reason she was provided a spot right out of the academy to bank fraud squad was because the agency placed little emphasis on casework, and all its attention to its very important and highly visible protective mission; thus, senior management saw nothing wrong with this decision so long as the agent would not be involved in a high-profile protective mission. Since they were uncertain or lacked confidence in her abilities, they protected her by placing her in a sought-after, white-collar, sit-behind-your-desk-type of squad. The problem with this decision is bank fraud at the time was a premier spot in the white-collar crime arena and should have been given to someone who was worthy of such a spot. In the grand view, this is a trivial example, but yet, very revealing to how, in general, government works. Usually ignoring an issue is the path chosen, rather than addressing it head-on.

I grabbed the general details from her, and after hanging up the phone, I immediately called the contact. The person who was making the complaint was the head of security of a firm in midtown Manhattan. I recall his first name was John. So John explained the situation to me and provided details, as he knew them. Basically, an employee who worked in one of tenant offices at the building had his personal mail stolen. He apparently did not receive his federal tax refund check, which was scheduled to arrive 4 days prior, and it had been deposited into an account not belonging to the victim. I remember ascertaining further details surrounding the time frame and information provided to the victim by the Internal Revenue Service.

The victim apparently had explained to John that the refund check was recently mailed and negotiated. I then called the United States Postal Inspection Service and confirmed that the check was, in fact, delivered 4 days prior. All incoming mail was registered and recorded and the check in question was recorded as received at the mailroom. I then asked John if he could pull the schedule and tell me who was working in the mailroom at the time the check was delivered to the mailroom. He responded, "Everyone." There was one exception. An employee who was out on medical leave and did not report to work due to a foot injury sustained prior to this issue of the stolen check that had surfaced. I informed John to hold everyone in the mailroom; not to let them go home. I spontaneously, without having thought about it, said, "Tell them this is a national security issue and that the Secret Service is on the way to question everyone." I was on my way . . .

Now there was one piece of information John did not get from the victim, but rather, he obtained it from an unrelated investigation being conducted by the FBI-NYPD Joint Robbery Task Force. Apparently, they were investigating a woman, Rachelle Commodore, who was a teller at the European American Bank, EAB. This bank had been held up at gunpoint on three separate occasions. It was located near the United Nations. Rachelle's boyfriend, my soon-to-be subject, Adrian Carne, worked in the mailroom at the security firm. As soon as John finished his briefing of the unsolved bank robbery, I informed him that I wanted to interview Adrian last.

I headed to the street and jumped into my unmarked police vehicle, a black Firebird with undercover license plates, and drove uptown to meet John and interview each individual, one at a time, in one of the empty mailroom offices. I kept them all for about 30 minutes, asking all sorts of questions that had nothing to do with the real reason I was there, but I was setting up the stage and the theme of my play. I needed it all to work. Of course, once we got to the subject, the person I believed stole the check, things would change. I am at the mailroom and just finished interviewing everyone except the person I was there for . . .

Adrian, a young, thin, tall, black male, entered the room. I introduced myself. "Hi, my name is Nino Perrotta. I'm a special agent with the United States Secret Service. Do you know why I am here?" He responded, "Yeah, huh, somebody threatened the president." *OK,* I thought to myself, *we have another "mameluke" here* . . . I immediately corrected him and went into my creative explanation, "No no no . . . son, no . . . That's what I told your friends in order to protect you. You see, the Secret Service has a lot of satellites, and we are constantly watching people who may be of interest to us. We also protect the money and all federal checks from being compromised, or, in this case, stolen. Would you like me to show you at my office the video we were able to collect from our satellites of you taking a check last week from this mailroom in the amount of $17,000?"

Instantly, his head tilted downward, an all-too-often recognizable sign that he was ready to cooperate. At that moment, only a trained investigator can tell that the subject is ready to take the next step. I told him, "You know we can fix this issue, but I will need you to cooperate with me." A bit confused and afraid of the consequences, Adrian ultimately began cooperating by telling me how his girlfriend at the bank was the one who forced him to do it, and that they have a baby together, and he loves her. I responded by saying, "Listen to me, show me you want this to be behind you. You make a call to her and all you need to say is that you have another check for her."

He agreed, and from the office with my little black bag of technical goods, he made the recorded call to Rachelle. She didn't necessarily bite all the way, BUT, she did agree to discuss the check once he came home. The subject has already waived his rights, signed his confession statement, and agreed to cooperate in the hope he does not face jail time. Of course, I would never promise anyone they would not go to jail. I did it! I was filled with confidence in myself and eager to make a federal case from a tip that a coworker was too busy to handle. So with my black leather jacket and worn, often mocked but comfortable black biker boots, I had successfully met a suspect, got him to confess to stealing the check, and implicated his girlfriend, the mother of his child. Most importantly of all, it looked like I was about to come face-to-face with the FBI, and little did I know that I would soon join yet another task force.

I told Adrian to keep this situation confidential and to beep me if he had any issues. Back in the day, before cell phones, we used Skytel 2-way pagers. I needed to head back to the office to make all of my notifications. While I was typing away, the phone rang. I answered it, and on the other end was a bubbly man who identified himself as Tom Buda, a detective with the NYPD. All was fine with the conversation . . . until he said he was with the FBI Joint Robbery Task Force. *The FBI? What do they want? I thought.* Well, to be fair, Buda did explain that John, the head of security, had just left his office and relayed the outcome of my case with Detective Buda. Buda also shared with me the facts of an unsolved bank robbery he was working on and how their main subject was Adrian's girlfriend, Rachelle Commodore. Commodore was a short, heavyset, African American young woman who was born in 1973. She worked as a bank teller at the European American Bank, EAB, near the United Nations, and lived on Convent Avenue in Manhattan.

Apparently, Tom, who was working on an unsolved armed bank robbery case with his partner, a very seasoned special agent by the name of Walter Carroll, had Adrian's "girlfriend" Rachelle under investigation. The Southern District of New York Bank Fraud section assigned Assistant United States Attorney Mark Godsey who was also handling my bank fraud investigation for the stolen check. Mark was young, clean-shaven, and new to the U.S. Attorney's Office. He enjoyed the combination of working with the three agencies, and I, in particular, saw great value in someone who was both genuinely interested in solving cases and prosecution. Mark was a smart attorney who had a great demeanor, cool and calm, and I eventually got to work with him on an undercover investigation that I initiated, targeting several key players that were still in the prepaid calling card business and defrauding carriers and the general public.

In any event, Tom and Walter were looking into Rachelle, an EAB bank teller that was let go due to the suspicious circumstances surrounding three armed bank robberies. Rachelle became a key suspect who the FBI believed participated with a group of Rastafarian thugs who had successfully pulled off three separate armed bank robberies at the same branch where Rachelle had at one time worked. Walter and Tommy had grown increasingly frustrated since all of their leads were hitting dead ends. Although I was already a bit "tainted" about working with the FBI, I grew to respect and admire Agent Carroll almost immediately. With regards to work ethic and tenacity, we had a great deal in common. With regards to personality and people skills, Tommy and I were very similar. Walter was the poster child for the FBI. A typical FBI agent, which was noticeable by the way he dressed, to his mannerisms, which were mild and a bit snooty to everyone outside the FBI arena. He was a soft-spoken man with a wife and children, all living in New Jersey; that's where the "typical" agent folks would live. New Jersey.

Anyway, Tommy was something else. He lived in Long Island, and his father was a very successful "high brass" in his day at NYPD. So, of course, Tommy was working a plum job due to his hooks and great personality. It was Carroll, on the other hand, who was not only a brilliant investigator but was also very calculated. Like a sponge, I soaked every word that came out of that man's mouth. Tommy first reached out to me, and he did a great job of breaking the ice. They wanted to meet, so I grabbed my jacket and ran over to FBI headquarters, which was walking distance from 7 WTC. I got there and was greeted first by Tommy and brought up to their office. NYPD was partnered up with FBI in what was called the FBI-NYPD Joint Robbery Task Force.

It is important to note that the Bank Robbery Task Force was formed in August 1979, and its main purpose was to investigate armed bank robbery violations in New York City and to apprehend those individuals responsible for committing these robberies. The task force memorandum outlined the confines by which the unit would operate, namely the four boroughs of Manhattan, Bronx, Brooklyn, and Queens. All cases handled by the task force were jointly investigated, with each task force team consisting of a police detective and an FBI agent.

During 1980, the first full year of the task force's operation, armed bank robberies in the city dropped to 252, compared to 319 in the preceding year. In February 2011, issues began to arise and chip away at this very effective unit. The NYPD, under the leadership of Commissioner Ray Kelly, at the time, was made up of over 35,000 police officers, and approximately 15,000 detectives withdrew their detectives from the task force. During my time working with the FBI-NYPD Joint Robbery Task Force, I found the command structure to be well established with clear operational guidelines as well as protocols in place. It was, what I believed, what a federal task force should look and feel like. It was a stark difference to what I was exposed to at the Secret Service; actually, it was absolutely nothing like what we had back at the office.

I was in a squad where both the supervisor and backup agent, usually a senior special agent, rotated in and out of positions in what appeared to be every 6 to 8 months. The experience level among the special agent investigators amounted to less than 1 year real-on-the-job experience. Actually, it was worse, when you take into consideration that most of us were only a few months out of the academy, with no field supervisor on hand. Our bosses knew less than what we knew, yet, somehow, we managed to make federal cases that stuck and no one got hurt. I am told that nowadays, the Secret Service has a very successful task force model and has a proven record of success in its financial fraud and cyber investigations as a result of its task forces. This makes me happy 'cause it is a different world out there today . . . so very different than the 1990s.

This exposure to the FBI was not only unique, but it provided me with a wonderful opportunity in both weighing and comparing my prior experiences, to both the Secret Service and the Joint Robbery Task Force. In a rare opportunity, I witnessed a hierarchy at the FBI that had a bit of arrogance toward the NYPD and often given less credit. However, in my opinion, NYPD were the "bread winners." When you think about it, it makes complete sense. The task force, for the most part, was filled with FBI agents from around the country. On the other hand, you have a local detective who knows the city, who was born in the city, who grew up on the very streets and among the people he now investigates. Who do you think will be more successful in obtaining a lead and cultivating rapport with a suspect or witness?

Once I arrived at the building, I was required to go through the typical security checks in place for the incoming general public. I found this a bit insulting since I had a gun and a badge like everyone else. Anyway, once I cleared the "square badge," there was Buda, standing there waiting for me. He was a tad shorter than me, with a mustache and a smile from ear to ear, fully animated. He was Italian, so we immediately hit it off. We got on the elevator to go see his FBI partner, Walter Carroll, who stood at about my height, 5 foot 8, thin frame, salt-and-pepper hair, clean shaven, with almost a baby face look to him. We slowly began to feel each other out, which was only natural. Walter was all FBI and immediately had to throw a dig at the Secret Service and said, "So, hey, when is your next protection assignment?" I responded, "Not sure since I'm off protection until a real agency solves this case." He laughed, and having each placed our "cards" on the table, in a manner of speaking, there were no hard feelings.

Unfortunately for the Secret Service, due to its primary mission of protecting the president, they did, in fact, have a reputation of running off in the middle of a case to do protection. This was well known among the law enforcement community, and it infuriated me personally. Yet, the FBI was nowhere near cracking the robbery case, and yet, despite the differences between the two agencies, my help was welcomed. Rachelle was a suspect in their robbery case; however, that case had gone cold as ice, and, at the time, seemed unbreakable. The girl responded to all questions with a frigid standard "NO." Denial seemed to be deeply embedded in her veins. Buda, although a qualified investigator and a smooth talker, she was totally on to him. Walter, on the other hand, was a thinker, deliberate when he spoke, but had no influence as well. Walter was all about investigative strategy and usually had Buda do the communication with suspects. So armed with little information other than a few photos collected from surveillance cameras at the bank, no other viable evidence was produced from their investigation. Again, Rachelle was their key suspect; however, they were unable to solve the armed bank robberies without her cooperation.

My case against Adrian who admitted to giving his girlfriend the stolen check breathed new life into the FBI-NYPD joint investigation. My case provided the potential hook into Rachelle, and soon after Adrian's confession, we joined forces, and I was able to collect additional information that placed Rachelle in the center of the stolen check case conspiracy. I was able to apply enough pressure for her to confess to her involvement. The collected information was powerful and condemning evidence. The stolen check had been deposited on or about December of 1996 into a fictitious bank account at European American Bank, EAB. This was same EAB branch where she at one time worked, and the same branch where all three bank robberies occurred.

Armed with this information, I knew exactly what to do and how to crack this cold case. I began engaging Rachelle almost daily, both in person and on the telephone. I was extremely carefully not to press too hard, so as to gain her trust and confidence. On the afternoon of February 10, 1997, I drove my unmarked police car, the same I did the night I responded to the tip and picked Rachelle up at her residence on Convent Avenue. I made an important stop before getting to her apartment. I picked up three Italian subs, one for her, one for the female agent who was required to be present whenever transporting a female, and one for me. Armed with the sandwiches, Rachel came down and got in the car. We ate them on the drive downtown to the New York Field Office at 7 World Trade Center.

As I approached the building, I radioed the Secret Service dispatcher who then notified building security, and without hesitation, these massive steel garage doors open. We then slowly pull inside in my unmarked vehicle. Rachelle laughed the entire way down to my office and even during the booking process continued to make jokes and laugh. I read her the Miranda rights, she waived them by signing the forms, and off we went to the next step. As we photographed and fingerprinted her, I made sure that no one either offended her or treated her disrespectfully. In law enforcement, mostly due to frustration, agents would make smart-ass remarks to "perps." I wanted to avoid that since the woman had gone through a great deal in her life, living in Harlem under very tough conditions, a single parent for the most part, and potentially looking at some serious jail time. Also, the last thing I wanted was for her to feel I was against her and the potential opportunity of having her cooperate on the bank robberies would never happen.

Well, the gentle process, kind gestures, and Italian sub sandwich worked in my favor. It eventually worked for the robbery case as well. We were about to take her to the Southern District of New York where the U.S. Marshal Service would take custody. She gestured to me that she had something to tell me about the bank robberies. I took her into the interview room where she provided me the outline of her involvement and that of others. That afternoon, Rachelle provided her version of her involvement with the stolen check case. It didn't matter how truthful she was with my case, with her statement, that of Adrian's, and all the other evidence collected; we had enough to arrest her and convict her, if needed, but her check case confession became the grease that finally loosened her lips. As soon as she gave me her written confession of the stolen check, Tom Buda was waiting for my call to come over to 7 World Trade Center and take the confession regarding the bank robberies. The look on Rachelle when Tom entered the room was hilarious. For some reason she wanted nothing to do with him and made it clear once he showed up. But in a matter of minutes, I was able to calm her down and convince her this was the best thing she could do to get herself past this horrific situation.

She began to talk, but not without first giving Buda a long dirty look that made me smirk. Her story began with a man she identified as Kiki and how he entered the bank with her agreeing to give him the best times to arrive and initiate their scheme. She explained the steps on how they planned the robberies and how they argued over money and how, during one of the robberies, Kiki had waved a gun in Rachelle's face. She was pissed at the time and during the confession, she explained the act of waving a gun in her face was totally disrespectful. Notwithstanding all the drama from Rachelle, we had the confessions, and we were now focused on identifying the other suspects.

Once Rachelle confessed to her involvement, she made the pivot to basically becoming my informant. I then switched my attention toward identifying some of the other bank robbers that Rachelle did not know and were only identified by their photos taken by bank surveillance. So I began reviewing phone toll records that Tom and Walter had requested for the case. Toll records are basically voluminous lists of telephone calls, both incoming and outgoing, that are made from a particular phone and within a billing cycle. When I was at OCTF, I was constantly reviewing phone records since I believed a phone, especially a cell phone, was almost like a fingerprint left at a crime scene. Each phone user had their distinctive habits and patterns, and I looked for those patterns back then and now in this investigation.

I immediately subpoenaed all the records during each month before and after all three of the armed robberies. The goal was to identify the bank robbers and begin to put together their inner circle. We knew that Rachelle was involved because during all three robberies, the one constant was the fact that she was working. So, perhaps, there was a telephone call made by someone to either her landline at the bank or to her cell phone directly. I was looking for something that would produce a potential lead, and better yet, even a suspect.

None of this really mattered unless, as Walter believed we could, we snatched one of the suspects and get them to confess. This was an approach with merit, yes, but the one I favored was the one which would apply a bit more pressure on the person with the most to lose. Tom and Walter both agreed, we needed to turn the screws a bit on Rachelle. She had a baby and was never arrested. Although the phone records produced a very important lead, in the end, however, it was Rachelle who gave everyone the break they were looking for.

At a very suspicious time, approximately minutes prior to one of the robberies, a call was made to Rachelle's cell phone. It came from another bank not far from the EAB bank. Armed with the surveillance photos assembled together as part of the public awareness flyer circulated throughout New York City, Tom and I headed to see if there were any potential leads. We were at the branch no more than 5 minutes asking general questions when an employee identified one of the suspects as a man who worked in the mailroom. The guy left the job a week prior to our visit. We were excited. This was the result of classic investigative work. The actual bank robbers were career criminals, all young men with a violent criminal past. They were part of a Rastafarian crime group operating in Manhattan and Brooklyn.

A peculiar aspect of this case took place prior to my direct involvement in its actual investigation. I had been working a protection assignment at a hotel only a few blocks away from the EAB bank that was robbed. It was actually robbed during the time we were armed and protecting a foreign dignitary at the hotel. The very next day, while reading the local newspaper, the armed bank robbery article caught my attention. I remember bringing the article into work and sharing the incident with my friends in the squad.

The incident was extremely interesting to me since the hotel was flooded with both special agents and NYPD detectives, all armed to the teeth, and yet no one was informed of the incident, not even by radio. Why did this all occur without any warning? I mean, we had NYPD assigned to the protective details, so certainly they were aware of the radio calls, and we had protective intelligence teams in the area. What information did they miss or not receive? I was very upset that all the while we, the Secret Service, were protecting dignitaries, yet across the street an armed bank robbery had successfully taken place and the bad guys got away without incident.

This is absolutely crazy. As I write this, I once again grow frustrated thinking of the potential impact such an occurrence could have on a protective detail. What is the average time from the moment a silent alarm is mobilized for police response to occur? We had police in plainclothes and in uniform less than 100 yards away from the incident. What if one of the bank robbers decided to take hostages, and what if one of our protectees decided to walk across the street at the same time the robbery took place to get money? Sometimes, successful execution of the protective mission, although reliant on comprehensive advance work, thorough, and professional execution of security protocols . . . sometimes, it just comes down to timing and a little good luck.

Tom was dumbfounded by Rachelle's level of cooperation with me. One day, he asked her why she finally decided to cooperate with the investigation. With an almost immediate and expressionless response, she replied, "You guys were assholes, and Nino was so kind and gentle with me." She then asked Tom to find me. Her statement flattered me, and more importantly, this was a great opportunity for me. The success of this case . . . getting all the culprits who had armed weapons and who were dangerous off the street . . . was an honor.

The details of the case spread through the Secret Service field office like wildfire. My supervisor, the unpopular one, acted as if he was a groupie and placed me on a pedestal. I was embarrassed. It made me feel very uncomfortable. It was not what I wanted. I was already very busy working cases, looking for my next target, and was not interested in the fluff. I was given an on-the-spot award for my achievements, and soon, I had agents like Frank, whose last name will remain unmentioned, chasing me around the office and looking for me during my early-morning runs on the West Side Highway asking questions about how I conducted my investigations and bragging about his arrest counts.

I remember thinking, as I increased my speed slowly leaving him behind me, what the fuck is this mameluke talking about? Internally, I questioned him, *Dude, it is not about the number of arrests you make; it needs to be all about the number of convictions. Thus, if you're not working alongside the prosecutor and identifying a network as opposed to a smash-and-grab case which is more of a local authority street crime approach, we, the Secret Service, should not be doing it.*

Our job was not street crime, and we need to elevate ourselves to what a special agent should be. Anyway, I began to alter my workout routine so to avoid this well intended agent's questions, but this became the norm for me. So to hear folks like Frank tell me they have all these arrests, basically of drug users or homeless folks steeling Treasury checks from a mailbox, was not impressive at all. We are the Secret Service, I thought, and although protecting the integrity of the mail system and federally issued checks was important, we needed to elevate ourselves and look at the bigger picture.

Prior to joining the Secret Service, my personal experience in dealing with the FBI was very limited. Most, if not all, of the "rhetoric" about the FBI came from the retired NYPD guys that worked at the New York State Organized Crime Task Force (OCTF). There was a great deal of animosity toward the Bureau, and it was understandable due to the history between the two organizations. Echo could not stand them, and Vincent Heintz, being newly exposed to them, was somewhat cautious and unimpressed. As explained earlier, I had very limited exposure to them, and everything up to now that I knew about the FBI was from the true crime books I read and what was shared to me by both Vince and Echo who were battling with the FBI White Plains Office. It wasn't until shortly after the Commodore case did I truly understand their arrogance and sense of entitlement toward cases, especially those cases associated with the Mafia. My experience with

Walter and Tom may have been an anomaly, but the success that comes from such cooperation was obvious. Nonetheless, the bank robbery case was now behind me, and it wasn't long that I got a true firsthand experience of the "controlling" and narcissistic FBI that folks like Echo warned me about.

Within months after the successful outcome of the bank robbery case, I identified key Mafia targets and had obtained court orders through Vince, Carroll, and Margie, who were the prosecuting team, for a series of new pen registers. It was clear I had begun to "shake" the Gambino crime family tree once again, and now certain FBI agents saw my aggressive investigative approach as stomping on their turf. It soon became a personal battle. No sooner after poking at a few wise guys, now with a Secret Service badge, I had my first dealings with the FBI, the "infamous" C-16 Squad. This once elite organized crime squad, dedicated to solely investigating the Gambino crime family, today, has been reduced to almost nonexistent levels.

Like so many other programs today that have been either reduced or replaced with both counterintelligence and terrorism squads, this one-time elite and specialized unit had more than 60 full-time agents. I recall a phone call one day where a female agent, her name was Stacy, identified herself as FBI. She called and began to inquire about a subpoena I served on a mobster called Salvatore "Fat Sal" Scala earlier that day. I thought this call out of the blue was quite odd. Anyway, she continued, and I was able to understand from the way she was speaking that she was interested in finding out more on what I was investigating rather than coordinating our efforts. But the way she inquired about Scala was as if she owned him. I responded by telling her the truth. I said, "Stacy, look, my interests in Scala are part of a grand jury investigation, and thus, it is all confidential, and I am so sorry, but I can't relay those details to you."

Although I was polite, I could tell I had truly pissed her off, but I was not the NYPD nor OCTF. I was the Secret Service, a special agent like her, and that meant I had "some" whack. The call immediately ended with a polite exchange.

Now, I mention the NYPD and OCTF since the history of the turf wars among them and the FBI were like no other turf battles ever fought in law enforcement. They were history and intense battles over jurisdiction and cases. The FBI treated wise guys who were cooperating like high-end real estate, and to them, the locals such as the NYPD and OCTF were all corrupt.

Hey, although I didn't like it, I basically ignored them. These types of cases were the ones that paved the path for government attorneys toward high-paying private law firms and rewarded the FBI agents who were a part of it, with promotions and coveted assignments. So, based on advancing their public exposure and protecting their interests, the FBI had successfully perfected the formula to ensure both—a formula that pinned politics over justice, federal criminal law over prosecution, and an unhealthy mistrust in everyone, including those of us who worked hard each day to arrest bad people regardless of association.

Following my C-16 experience, I now had to contend with the FBI, White Plains Office, since they were working on Gotti Junior and his involvement in an extortion case from the owners of the Scores strip club. The FBI agents assigned to that investigation were Bill and Jack. As an important side note, between March of 1994 through February 1997, OCTF and the Bronx DA's office conducted a joint investigation, with the cooperation of NYPD's Vice Enforcement and Major Case Squads, the Office of the Inspector General of the School Construction Authority, and the United States Attorney's Office for the

Southern District of New York. In the latter part of 1997, the United States Secret Service developed a body of evidence relating to telecommunication fraud collected during the state investigation.

With OCTF's assistance, the FBI, in late 1996, conducted a separate investigation, which produced evidence to be used in the prosecution of certain common subjects. Sometime during my Secret Service academy training there was a decision, one that Echo and I regret to this day. It was the decision to move the case to the federal level as opposed to keeping it at the state. Vince and senior officials at OCTF decided to take the case to the federal level due to at the time concerns over a recent ruling with regards to the use of state pen registers. The concern came with the Court of Appeals February 25, 1993, decision, *People v Bialostok* (80 N.Y. 2d 738). The decision stated the following: "a pen register, capable of monitoring conversations, should be treated as an eavesdropping device subject to the warrant requirements specified in the criminal procedure code, notwithstanding that the audio function was disabled or that no conversations were actually seized."

Vince was concerned with this decision, and thus, since it was not an issue in federal court, this concern helped influence his decision to take the case at the federal level. Soon after the switch and meeting federal prosecutors, Vince and Echo were introduced and assured that Bill and Jack would play respectfully "in the sandbox" and thus, since they were working on a case involving similar subjects who were involved with extorting a strip club known as Scores, they should compare notes and work with each other. Echo will tell you that this was a very bad move and that after providing them a recorded conversation that involved proof of Scores being extorted, Echo couldn't shake the two agents off his back and that of the OCTF investigation. So, while I was working on the Commodore case, I would often hear about the turf battles and arguments, and those battles basically drove Echo to desperately find a solution, one that eventually involved bringing the Secret Service into the fold.

I stayed in close contact with Vince Heintz. I was the godfather to his son Dan, who is, today, a hulking young man, and seeing my own son now grow like a weed, I truly regret not seeing Dan grow up. At the time, I was all over the world with the Secret Service so I got very little wiggle room or free time. Anyway, Vince and I stayed in touch, and one day, after giving him an overview of my caseload, we both concluded, with a short laugh, and he would say, "Come on, what was more exciting as well as challenging than to investigate the New York mob?" The joking reference immediately sobered me, and our conversation immediately switched from my caseload in the Secret Service to where they were with the Gotti investigation. He would start with praising me for my past work that was characterized as a tenacious investigative style, and then lay out the issues they were having with the White Plains FBI and how Echo was so increasingly frustrated with them, that Vince was actually concerned for his health.

The FBI agent Jack looked like the early version of Clark Kent, Superman's pseudo identity, while his partner, Bill, looked a bit like what you would guess a real-life "mameluke" of a guy would look like. I was waiting for these two since Echo had complained about them to me almost regularly. They were your typical 100 percent FBI agents. You could spot them from a mile away. They were only concerned with taking over cases, promoting the FBI, and leaving you out to dry. Although Echo hated the Bureau, he and Vince had no choice but to bring them in on the case due to the legal arguments presented on the state level. Thus, it was a decision that weighed heavily to this day for Echo. We recently chatted, and we both admitted that there is not a day that passes that we don't think about the case and dumb politics and turf wars that went on. Echo will tell you he knew from the very first meeting with the two that they were not team players.

On September 26, 1997, at approximately 4:30 p.m., I received a call from Special Agent Jack. After beating around the bush, he asked about my conversations with another FBI agent who was working at the NYC office. I responded by telling him that my prepaid calling card case was focusing on Denny McLain and that I was trying to make contact with the agent who had investigated McLain for defrauding the Peet Packing Company. Immediately, he went into how he was offended and that I needed to go through him since this was his case, and at that moment, I stopped him. I corrected him and told him, "Look, this is a Secret Service case, and I am working in conjunction with the NY State OCTF, not the FBI." Also, I said to Jack, "If you are offended by me not calling you, how about your C-16 squad calling me and asking who were my targets as if they had right to that information?" We screamed and yelled like there was no other, and the conversation ended with one of us hanging up. My next call was to Vince and his Assistant United States Attorney, (AUSA) partners. The battle had begun . . .

That recent decision associated with the use of pen registers was what put Vince and the case in a difficult position. Under NYS law, there was an equivalent of the RICO statue on the books that was called Enterprise Corruption Statue, which was added to the Organized Crime Control Act of 1986. So like RICO, it allowed you to basically stitch together criminality, going back many years if needed from various crimes like bank fraud, mail fraud, loan sharking, extortion, and murder, and put them all in to one case. Each crime was identified as a predicate act, and two or more provided you the basis for RICO. So with these predicate acts and having the syndicate order them, which was your job to prove—basically bridge a gap that, at one time, was impossible for law enforcement/prosecutors to do.

What you had in practice prior to RICO or on the NY state level Enterprise Corruption, the guy (Boss/Capo/Soldier) that ordered someone to commit the crime was exempt from trial. RICO/Enterprise Corruption focused on the layers of the Mafia. But with all these similarities on the state level, Vince was concerned about the defense possibly challenging the pen registers used, and this was a nonissue on the federal level. The concern was that if the defense could legally argue and successfully get the pen registers excluded, in essence, all the evidence produced from the pens for the entire case would be thrown out. SHIT, the entire case was built on investigative steps of gradual progression. Unlike the FBI, we stayed away, for the most part, in using snitches/CIs to then wires. So if the pens get excluded, so do the electronic eavesdropping . . . Now I was in the academy in Glynco, Georgia, at the time this relationship occurred between OCTF and the FBI.

Similar to how an army cadence would go but with a bit of "flavor" added, "Here we go again, same old shit again" . . . Anyway, so the decision although I was aware of it, I personally had nothing to counter it with since it all played with the goal of moving the case federally and away from the potential pen register issues. Later, Vince would repeatedly, as well as Echo on separate occasions, wish I could join them as a Secret Service agent, but at that particular time, although my 1995 affidavit expanded the reach of the wiretaps to now Gotti Junior and others, what was intercepted/collected that would later be the PHONE CARD CASE, was just too premature and outside anyone's scope, including mine. In hindsight, Vince stated on numerous occasions how he wished he never did it, bring the FBI to the table as well as going federal. Echo went along with it, with not much pushback. He was always supportive to whenever Vince proposed a legal strategy, but his gut was not to do it. He once said to me, "Hey, what the fuck! How much worse could we be if we were challenged by the defense? At the very least, we knew who the enemy was . . ."

Here is Nino Perrotta in an after action at West Point, New York during his Fordham Army ROTC days some time in 1988-89. Nino's determination and dedication can be seen all over his face.

The United States Attorney for the Southern District of New York, serving from 1993 to 2002; Mary Jo White, Special Agent Walter Carroll, FBI, Detective Tom Buda NYPD and Special Agent Nino Perrotta, United States Secret Service. We are all at SDNY receiving awards for the Cammodore Investigation.

A photo of me (Special Agent Nino Perrotta) going to work (7 WTC) in 1997 with my government "G" ride, a black firebird.

Here is a photo of Special Agent Nino Perrotta, ATSAIC Robert Weaver and Special Agent Chris Funk. If you look closely, I'm jokingly cuffing Weaver and we had just completed a successful undercover operation against a mob associate "Eli" who was involved in the prepaid phone card business with both the Gambino and Genovese Crime family.

This is the building where John Gotti "Junior" ran his prepaid phone card business. The picture was taken on October 7, 1997 and it captured ATSAIC Marty Walsh and SA Nino Perrotta, United States Secret Service as they were exiting the Gotti location. There is also a picture of the thousands of printed Liberty Tell phone cards seized from the search.

In this picture also taken on October 7, 1997, you see Jack Shaughnessy seated at the table, ATSAIC Robert Weaver discussing the evidence with SA Nino Perrotta and other members of the search warrant team in the back drop.

Search warrant in Florida and we seized more Gotti "Junior" prepaid phone cards; Liberty Tel.

A consent search in Brooklyn presented more worthless prepaid calling cards that the mobsters wanted to activate in the near future.

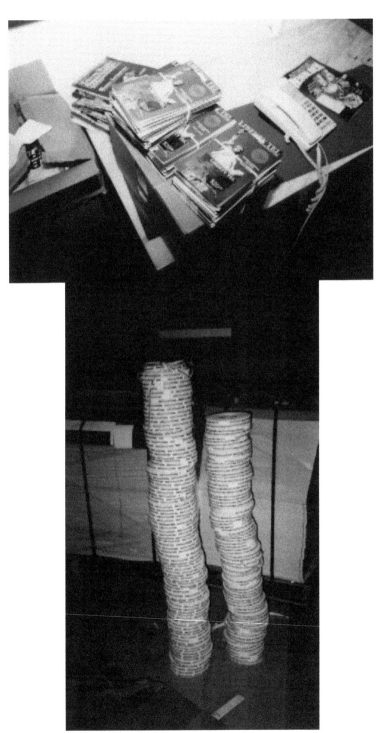

Search warrant in Florida where we seized PIN numbers and more Liberty Tel prepaid calling cards.

Here is a photo we took at a ceremony acknowledging various law enforcement folks for their individual investigative accomplishments. We were on the USS Intrepid and in the photo to the left is SAIC Brian Gimlett and far right DSAIC Chip Smith. My mom and dad are both flanking me. It was a proud moment being publicly recognized for my contribution towards the Gotti "Junior" investigation.

7

Let's Slide in
Those Phone Cards!

To be clear and to be fair, this criminal act, identified as an unknown fraud scheme, was investigated and the seeds of the scheme flushed out only after the wiretaps ceased to operate. There was no development, interviewing, or other investigative steps taken while the interceptions were collected, and it was my job to re-create the "crime scene."

18/07/1996

Nagib C. wrote:

"So, my question to the Sclers out there, did any of you try these Conetco prepaid cards, and if so, how is your experience with it? If not, be aware, indeed, I lost $40, but I hate for anybody else to lose any more money if it is a SCAM."

"Nagib, I used these cards for the past 2 years. And trust me, it was less than 79 cents a minute. The company is out of business. Why? It's a long story; someone made millions. Anyway,

a new company will start soon, and they will refund any un-opened card. Sorry, Nagib, you joined the wagon at the end of the trip. You lost $40, but others lost thousands. As for Sege El Khazen, I'm sure he has nothing to do with it. He lost money as you did."

Please reply, Nagib C.

Click here to Reply, Nagib C.

18/07/1996

"This message is to share information with the rest of you. A month ago, I saw the ad for calls to Lebanon for $.79 a minute. I went ahead and bought two of them from Mr. El K., thinking that everything is legit. When I got the cards. I tried them and was kind of disappointed with the charges since it did not match with the time spent. For example, I talked for 10 minutes and got charged for 14. So like a sucker, I went ahead and paid for them since the total amount was not worth re-turning them and paid more postage on top of the whole thing. So I kept them to finish them later. I had 31 minutes left. However, I have been trying calling their 800 number for the last month and was never able to get connected after that.

"The funny thing is, I contacted Mr. K back and the following was his answer."

> *"Hello, N,*
>
> *"I received your e-mail and here is my response. First of all, I am just responsible for selling cards. I am not responsible for the timing and the rates and how to*

connect. The rate on the cards I sent you was 79c/min to Lebanon, and the timing is done by the computer and is the same as AT&T timing. I ask everybody to use the cards before they send me the money to make sure that I am not trying to rip them off, and I asked you to use the cards before you send me the money. All what I do is buying cards from wholesale and selling them within their pricing value. And I do not own or operate those companies. So if you have a problem with them, you can call their customer service and complain. Anyway, if you still have a card unopened, I will send you a refund.

"Regards, Serge El-K"

These are some of the complaints from consumers as well as one reseller's response. All these complaints are still available online. These communications are associated with the prepaid calling cards that were sold on or about the time the scheme to defraud consumers via prepaid calling cards was at its peak. The intercepts from OCTF wiretaps were recording John Gotti Junior describe his intentions to his driver Anthony Plomitallo.

During my investigation into the fraud, folks who began to hear about the investigation would begin to mail me their complaint letters with their now defunct and worthless phone cards enclosed. All of the letters I received had a common theme, similar to the online complaints cited; the consumer had purchased phone cards, and without warning, these cards either stopped working and/or the cards cheated them out of phone time. This was an ingenious way to defraud unsuspecting consumers. Soon, many people in the industry who either made a living selling prepaid calling cards or were involved with "stoking" the scheme, or simply tried cleaning the industry from its terrible reputation, began to reach out to me. I had more cooperating witnesses on this case than on any other case combined.

Some of these people were real "characters," especially the ones who profited in selling shady prepaid calling cards and now wanted to co-operate in hopes they would not be indicted. My dealings with them were, at times, quiet amusing. Their general demeanor and how they "rationalized" their actions were filled with an element of comedy. Although their identities today still need to be kept confidential, I was amazed at how small that community was and how much they knew about each other. Now, the fraud committed was certainly not funny or something to make light of, however, because many had never seen or spoken to a Secret Service agent; they were worried. Some were even a bit "starstruck" at first and wanted to impress me with their knowledge and provided information in hopes to meet me and my colleagues so as to brag that they had rubbed shoulders with the Secret Service.

They all hoped that once connecting with me, they might be privy to gossip about the president or first lady, which, of course, never hap-pened. In any event, they all provided bits and pieces of information related to the prepaid calling card puzzle, and as I entertained them and their curiosity, I emerged, eventually, as an expert in the field. Once I accumulated all that was available from the "streets," under-standing every angle and various schemes associated with the prepaid calling card business, I would bring those cooperating witnesses, one by one, into the Secret Service field office for an interview. It was then they realized for the first time that the gig was up.

I received my first break with an attorney who worked for AT&T. The attorney's name was Meric Bloch. Meric was amazing, and we are still great friends today. He patiently provided details and information on the telecommunications industry; specifically, the prepaid calling card business, and he helped me formulate the "hypothesis" associated with the fraud scheme. He was always there for Special Assistant United States Attorney Vince Heintz, as he had specific questions geared toward the industry. At every call, and there were so many of those, Meric, an AT&T corporate attorney, was always ready to provide me with the information, answering my questions or at times, he was there helping me understand the business side of the prepaid calling card industry.

As I continued to review the transcripts of the intercepted conversations, had my daily conversations with Meric, and interviewed scores of witnesses, some of whom were eventually converted to cooperating witnesses, I was beginning to formulate a common "theme" to the fraud scheme. It was very similar to a typical Mafia "bust out" scheme, but in this case, everyone was in on it. The victims were telecommunications giants and the less fortunate consumers who needed to purchase prepaid calling cards to call family in foreign countries. Also, a traditional bust out scheme had one main victim who was typically someone in debt to the mob and who owned a business. That business was collateral and a vehicle for the mob to purchase merchandise using the owner's credit. That merchandise was quickly liquidated for cash. Since there was no intent in ever paying back the suppliers, the victim was forced into bankruptcy and financial ruin.

As I continued to peel away at the investigation, it was clear that we needed to determine an approximate dollar amount of prepaid calling cards printed and try to compare it to the international time contracted to resellers like Tel Central, Denny McLain's company. What would be ideal was to make a connection that a conspiracy to commit fraud existed. It was too early to tell, but soon, that conspiracy was not only present but frozen on an intercepted conversation.

In most instances, a conspiracy charge would be corroborated through a confidential informant who, if credible, would be asked to testify in court, or potentially, he/she would wear a wire to obtain the necessary proof. But after reviewing all the intercepted conversations, hundreds of hours' worth, and then finding that one conversation where Gotti described the fraud scheme in his own words, the groundwork was set in tying the Gambino crime family, the syndicate, to a conspiracy became a reality, and the reliance on a confidential informant was absolutely not necessary.

I knew I had to approach this case in a much different manner than if I was present working at the "plant", actively listening to the conversations in real time. If I was actually listening to the conversations, my approach would have been the following: identify both old and new targets who were participants in the scheme, build the probable cause to draft the affidavits for additional wiretaps targeting the new targets, their locations, mobile devices, and vehicles used by the new targets, conduct active surveillance in several new locations within New York State, including crossing state lines in places like Florida and Michigan. Once those wiretaps and surveillance teams were comfortable with their respective duties, I would execute in a timely manner strategic search warrants with several goals, such as tickling the bugs for a response, seizing cash, and collecting any and all financial records available.

Instead, I had limited opportunity to do as I described; rather, I was forced to work with the collected intercepted conversations, identify "key" personnel in the industry who could help me answer some of the gaps present in the intercepts, spend numerous hours vetting information provided by the cooperating witnesses, and attempt to locate, if available, any and all proof and/or data that could provide evidence to the dollar amount of fraud committed by the scheme.

Whenever a search warrant seemed feasible, I creatively found ways to "update" the probable cause, and once that was accomplished, a warrant was issued and we went out to seize the evidence. Whenever a computer was seized, we would have the information on it analyzed and shared with the OCTF. Based on all the investigative steps taken, I came across a "main thug" who, although was indirectly associated to the conspiracy conversation that was intercepted in 1996 between Gotti Junior and Plomitallo, was, nonetheless, a main player who took the conspiracy beyond simply a conversation. That person was Denny McLain. The same McLain who, in 1968, became the last pitcher in major-league baseball to win 30 or more games during a season where he went 31–6, a feat that was accomplished by only 11 players in the twentieth century.

Denny McLain was born on March 29, 1944, in Markham, Illinois, and although he had an impressive baseball career, his downfall began very early during his professional career. In February 1970, *Sports Illustrated* and *Penthouse* magazines both published articles about McLain's involvement in bookmaking activities. In the *Sports Illustrated* article, an alleged source explained that McLain's foot injury suffered in late 1967 had been caused by an organized crime figure stomping on it for McLain's failure to pay money owed on a bet.

When I eventually located McLain, he was serving federal time for looting money from a pension fund tied to the workers of a company called Peet Packing Company located in Chesaning, Michigan. Within 18 months after the former baseball star and his partner, Roger Smigiel, purchased the business, it went bust. So in 1996, McLain was convicted of stealing $3 million from the company's pension fund in addition to money laundering, conspiracy, and mail fraud. It was alleged that both McLain and Smigiel were accused of using the money to pay company debts and personal expenses. When the company went under in June 1995, about 185 people lost their jobs at the plant. It didn't matter since, for Denny, even while he was having these issues, he continued to forge ahead with criminal activities and operated Tel Central, where he committed an even larger fraud.

Throughout the intercepted conversations, there were brief mentions of Denny McLain and Tel Central Communications, a reseller of international phone time which operated from 150 W. Jefferson, Detroit, Michigan. It was clear that Tel Central was important to the Liberty Tel prepaid calling card, which was owned by John Gotti Junior. As in every business, conversations center on efficiency, and in this case, we had intercepted the syndicate and the concern they had with McLain's equipment, in particular, the switches.

The switches are basically a term used to reference the system that allowed the phone cards that were purchased by the consumers to connect to the network access, the usage port that would allow them to make the international calls. It was basically the "highway" for phone traffic to flow. In addition to Denny being a topic of conversation, we heard another name, an individual by the name of Eli. Elias "M" of Brooklyn immediately became important to the case and eventually was made a target of the investigation since he was connected to both the earlier scheme with the Travel Card and now with Denny McLain; he was selling the Smile & Dial card.

As stated earlier, the Travel Card case was absorbed as part of my investigation, and I had information that pointed toward Eli and the group associated with Conetco. Therefore, Eli would eventually be interviewed and later was targeted through an undercover operation targeting him and his illegal business activities. Both his statements and the undercover operation proved to be a success and provided an understanding of the underground world and its involvement with the prepaid telecommunication industry.

Now, going back to the infamous May 28, 1996, intercepted conversations between Gotti and Plomitallo, we understood that Gotti did not want to see his plans disrupted as they had been for the Travel Card. With a little digging, it was understood the company behind the Travel phone card was Communications Network Corporation, otherwise known as Conetco. In that conversation, we heard Gotti discuss organizing national brokers and distributors so that they have total control of the distribution and the cards being sold. He explained then how Frank Cali, who reported to a Gambino mobster John D'Amico, would help them start up his own phone card in the same breath. Today, the current head of the Gambino crime family is Frank Cali. Cali was also a part of the Travel Card scam.

Conetco began selling phone cards in the summer of 1995, and by the spring of 1996, it was activating over $20 million worth of cards a month. When it went bankrupt late in 1996, it left WorldCom, the nation's No. 4 long-distance carrier, holding the bag for about $94 million. What was also known was that other reputed Gambino mobsters were tied to the firm, including Joseph (Joe the German) Watts and John (Jackie the Nose) D'Amico. Watts, who pleaded guilty in 1996 to disposing of a body in connection with a Gambino family slaying, allegedly was a mob "trailblazer" in phone scams. Within several sporadic intercepted conversations of Eli and Denny, I decided to find a "loose" spoke within this elaborate scheme.

I readily admit finding the connection and understanding the scheme was not easy. No one knew what we had, absolutely no one. In fact, as I mentioned earlier, the Manhattan DA's Squad immediately surrendered their case to me when they heard the Secret Service was investigating phones cards. There was no one in the Secret Service, no one in the FBI, and no one in the industry that was able to explain to me the actual fraud scheme. Yes, it is easy for someone to hear of the general scheme and say, "Oh yes, that is this," but in the end, it required an unprecedented consumption of investigative hours dedicated to slowly unraveling all of the pieces associated with the fraud, and then repackaging those pieces and categorizing the various steps associating the folks who committed them. The ultimate goal was proving "beyond a reasonable doubt" that they, in fact, committed the fraud. It was this part of the work I enjoyed most of all. I thrived in the meticulous and mundane details of figuring out the complexity and linking all the pieces together.

At first, I focused on the actual pin numbers that were associated with each prepaid card and found on the backside of the card. This led nowhere. Then as time went on, I attempted to associate the 800 number also found on the back of the card and used that to make a link, but it turned out to be a dead end as well. What eventually surfaced from all the probing, trial and error, was that the phone card had to belong to a company, a reseller of international phone time. The company needed a distribution network, which was what the Mafia provided. Now, in order to "expedite" the distribution of the cards, one would provide international calling time at a rate that was very cheap. The international long-distance rates sold to the consumer at the time were below market rate.

Therefore, firms like Tel Central and Conetco, who contracted with MCI and WorldCom upon signing contracts, ramped up their usage by selling the international time below market rates to prepaid calling card companies like Liberty Tell. It was obvious that the resellers of this international time like Denny McLain had no intention of paying the carrier "in full" because the formula of selling below the purchase price made no sense at all. Thus, selling international time below market rate made perfect sense only to folks like the ex-pitcher and to the Gambino crime family.

What helped me unravel the fraud scheme and was a "litmus test" came later with the interviews of Denny McLain's bookkeeper and mistress, and that of a "key" family member. Now what I didn't know at that time was that the FBI, in early 1997, basically at the same time I had started my investigation, interviewed people who shared information about the phone card business and how members of the New York syndicates were involved in the prepaid calling card business. The FBI had other interests and was focusing their attention on Walt Pavlo, a former employee of MCI. Pavlo, who has since been convicted, had created a scheme to defraud the fraudsters who had taken MCI for millions.

One such individual was Denny McLain who, through his firm, Tel Central, owed MCI approximately $30 million. Now, what would have been ideal was everyone on the good side working and sharing information to basically get the bad guys. That would have been the ideal situation. That option did not exist, however, and efforts were made for me not to receive any assistance from the FBI. This was shared in previous chapters, and in the end, my case suffered from such sabotage.

Anyway, it was clear through independent sources that Gene Lombardo, a member of the Bonanno crime family, was involved in the prepaid calling card business, and that he was receiving time for his cards from Tel Central Communications. Tel Central was Denny McLain's company, and he had an exclusive contract with MCI. Now, why was the FBI investigating prepaid calling cards basically at the same time I was? Well, the more important question was, why didn't the White Plains, FBI office, who Echo helped by sharing Scores evidence, return the favor? Because with the FBI, unfortunately, they make street signs that describe them, and those signs read: ONE WAY.

At the time, I looked for guidance and a layout of how the scheme worked, but no one had ever investigated anyone for this exact type of scheme, and thus, there were no prosecutions. The Manhattan DA had attempted to investigate Conetco Corporation, DBA Communication Network Corporation, which was located at 1 Penn Plaza, Suite 4311, New York, NY 10119. This reseller committed approximately $90 million of phone card fraud through the Travel prepaid calling card. Conetco was where John Gotti Junior had planned to take his business, but since they had busted and gone out of business, the OCTF wiretaps had secretly intercepted their plans to not do as Conetco did, but rather, be more versatile and fluid through Denny's firm, Tel Central.

In the end, Denny was already busting out MCI with other members of the Gambino crime family, and when he was eventually shut down, had committed well over 30 million in fraud. The Tel Central fraud was committed with cards like the MVP, Smile and Dial, and Liberty Tel. Now, Conetco, the "godfather" of prepaid calling card fraud, was owned by Vincent Rosillo and Al Khatib, and they had folks like Elias "M," Alphone "Allie Shades" Malangone, and Joe "the German" Watts, all either on the payroll or distributors of the prepaid cards. What is important to note is these folks were not just regular businesspeople; some were made members of the Mafia, and others associates, but in the end, I focused on potential targets who either spoke or were mentioned on the wiretaps.

For starters, Denny became a main target of the investigation, then to support his participation and activities we interviewed the bookkeeper, Elias and the family member who will go unnamed. Each and every one of these individuals I determined what role they would play. I would, of course, pitch the idea to Vince and Carroll, but in the end, they deferred to my judgment. So my first target was Paula. I recall the incident as if it was yesterday; I was in the Crown Plaza. It was during the annual United Nations General Assembly, also referred to as UNGA. It takes place every September and is a time when New York City hosts a multitude of foreign heads of states, each accompanied by large entourage, long motorcades, and gridlock abounds.

UNGA is a very important but busy time of the year in the city and especially for the Secret Service. All the heads of state around the world converge for 2 weeks at the United Nations for the general assembly. I was handed the assignment to secure the hotel where some of the most high-risk security details would be staying. The prime minister of Israel stayed at the hotel, and due to the high threat level against him, securing the hotel was no easy task and required long hours working alongside my NYPD partners. However, my main focus was fixated on the Mafia, and I would work on my case and make telephone calls while the diplomats were out conducting their own affairs.

Toward the end of my review and the investigative steps taken, I had not only developed extensive leads that provided confidential sources, some dirty, some almost dirty, and others who knew what they were but decided, smartly, to help me lay out the scheme, as well as point me in the right direction where both search warrants were executed, finding thousands of printed phones cards and storage facilities filled with worthless cards that had been shut down for nonpayment. When I inquired why the cards were kept, I was told the directive handed down was to hold on to those printed cards because they would be reused once reactivated.

Yes, can you believe it? They were that careless, and to the benefit of reconstructing the case, evidence was preserved, waiting for me to snatch it up. I remember hitting a storage facility and pulling out hundreds of boxes with thousands of prepaid cards in each. I recall the special agent in charge indirectly asking me how long we would have to store all the evidence, obviously concerned with the storage costs. Now remember, not everyone was dirty and not every distributor was connected to the scheme, but they all were part of the package, the package to move cards at a rapid rate when directed. So, since the Mafia controlled all the distribution, and everyone knew that if you didn't somehow participate, you and your business would pay for it, one way or another.

As I moved forward with the case and began to connect various dots, I would go back and reevaluate that "famous intercept" which was between Gotti Junior and Anthony Plomitallo. In that conversation, Gotti explained that what had occurred with the Travel Card and its unexpected demise would not happen with his Liberty Tel card because he would have numerous phone card companies already in place replacing any phone card that was turned off. So like a dam with a leak, he would be ready to plug the hole with another card. The intercepted conversation was the foundation that explained the plan to defraud, and the beauty of such an intercept provided me the ability to "connect" both the fraud committed by the Travel Card and Conetco, as well as the fraud committed by Liberty Tel, other prepaid calling cards, and Tel Central Communications.

Eventually, we charged Gotti and his associates with a conspiracy to commit fraud: 18 USC 1029, and if the case had gone to trial, all we needed to provide was evidence beyond a reasonable doubt that a conspiracy did take place. Nonetheless, my investigation in the phone card case continued to develop evidence. I collected evidence by interviewing new witnesses, developed "key" confidential informants, and a successful independent undercover operation against a key target.

The connection of Conetco and its questionable characters who were part of the syndicate, like Joe Watts and Allie Shades, to other "shady" folks connected to Tel Central like Denny McLain, Anthony Plomitallo, Michael Zambouros, and Gotti Junior, came from "drips and drabs" of conversations all from the initial wiretaps that Echo, scratching his head, brought over to the Secret Service. It all came into place later through the help of informants and cooperating witnesses that enabled me to realize that some of the folks who participated with the Conetco scam had moved on and were now involved with the Tel Central folks.

So when you talk about "sliding in," the phone cards were surely a slippery surprise to everyone. The case initially appeared to most like a typical organized crime case; no surprises and straightforward Mafia crimes. Who would have expected the presence of the Secret Service, and a fraud indictment that had "restitution" written all over it? I mean, even the defense attorneys were a bit puzzled and almost a bit out of their comfort zone when their clients had to face charges that were tied to a crime they had no idea how to defend. I mean, the Secret Service were considered the new guys on the block, and no one really knew anything about them. At the moment, the indictment rolled out, and we arrested everyone with the help of our local partners. Even though the FBI had also participated, you could see the concern in the eyes of every defendant.

8

Nic O Dan Communications & the Last of the Mohicans!

It was sometime in early 1997, and I was sitting in my new cubicle located in the credit card fraud squad. I was already working feverishly on my new cases. I had my regular load of credit card cases as well as the phone card case from OCTF now officially assigned to me; case number 108-779-235408-S/OC. ATSAIC Marty Walsh was my immediate supervisor. A quiet, no-nonsense type of a guy, a true New Yorker from Long Island. Thank God I finally had a boss who got the big picture. Marty was absolutely "old school," demanded respect, and dished respect out to hardworking agents. I immediately understood what he was all about and loved working for him. I had a tremendous amount of respect for Marty. The special agent in charge of the New York Field Office was a tall man with glasses and mustache named Brian F. Gimlet, and he provided me the berth I needed to work the case.

The Secret Service office had a daily buzz to it, and I was contributing to the busy tempo by working hard and continually building my reputation as a serious investigator. Marty, after a brief meeting in his office with his backup, essentially the number two, Gene Cunningham, a former counterassault guy who was an absolute gentleman, instructed me to work on the OCTF case. Initially, they wanted me not to include John Gotti Junior as a suspect on our memorandum reports. Marty and Gene agreed that they didn't want to attract too much attention to the case at its initial stages. It was a reasonable move since it isn't every day you target the head of an organized crime family as a Secret Service agent. In fact, I do not think it had ever been done before or since.

The early summer of 1996 had come and gone, starting with lots of post-standing assignments surrounding President Clinton's reelection campaign. A sample of these assignments included President Clinton's visit to Chicago, Illinois, on July 2, 1996, then some more post-standing assignments for the Summer Olympic Games in Atlanta, Georgia, followed with the August presidential bus campaign where I was part of a mobile site team, and that was followed up with the August 30, 1996, visit of President Clinton, Hillary Rodham Clinton, Vice President Albert Gore Jr., Mrs. Tipper Gore, and Chelsea Clinton to Cape Girardeau, Missouri, and Cairo. As explained earlier, these were just some of the assignments I was involved in, but it essentially made the summer months, the campaign year, and the winter inauguration seem as all one and the same. I somehow managed to fulfill these assignments with all of the associated travel, long hours, and juggled my investigative work, often while on some train, plane, or automobile en route to some town or airport.

Wow, I was finally where I wanted to be! After all the years of dreaming as a young child growing up in the family business, I was now on my way to hopefully joining the ranks of folks like DEA Special Agent Frank Panessa, who played a key role in the investigation that was called the "Pizza Connection" or FBI Special Agent Jules Bonavolonta who was credited in helping take down John Gotti Senior, and the very honorable Assistant United States Attorney Rudy Giuliani. It was Giuliani that had a very strong influence in my teenage life which helped encourage me as well as shape my desires to someday combat organized crime. Like him, for a period of time during my early adolescence, I believed in becoming a priest, I also attended a Bronx-based university, and while in college, majored, as he, in political science and minored in philosophy.

It was Giuliani's organized crime battles during the mid-'80s that amazed me. For example, in the "Mafia Commission Trial" that went from February 25, 1985, to November 19, 1986, Giuliani had indicted 11 organized crime figures, including the heads of New York's so-called Five Families, under the Racketeer Influenced and Corrupt Organizations Act (RICO) on charges that included extortion, labor racketeering, and murder for hire. Soon after, *Time* magazine called this the "Case of Cases" and possibly one of the most significant assaults on the infrastructure of organized crime since the high command of the Chicago Mafia was swept away in 1943.

Eight defendants were found guilty on all counts and subsequently sentenced on January 13, 1987, to hundreds of years of prison time. There eventually surfaced in an FBI memo, which was revealed about 20 years later, leaders of the five New York mob families voted in 1987 on whether to issue a contract for the death of U.S. Attorney Rudolph Giuliani. Heads of the Lucchese, Bonanno, and Genovese families rejected the idea, though Gambino leader John Gotti encouraged assassination. It was this information I would look for in all the New York papers and cut the articles out for keeps. Those articles and the agencies that helped investigate the Mafia got me hooked into becoming a federal agent.

It was July 25, 1997, when on "paper," I officially rejoined the OCTF case, but, in reality, I was working on it for several months prior in secrecy with the SAIC Gimlet's approval. I started diving into the "unknown" by reading the transcribed transcripts of the intercepted conversations. In order to identify any potential missed "signals," I read them once again while listening to the intercepted conversations. These were all the conversations that pertained to the Nic O Dan, Gotti's prepaid phone business, that he named after his two children at the time. The business was located in Queens, and the phone card Gotti personally owned was called Liberty Tel. It was a blue prepaid calling card with a picture of the Statue of Liberty.

So typically, the Mafia is always "way ahead" of law enforcement when it comes to schemes, but this advantage would soon change. With an unprecedented drive and with an almost obsessive focus to detail, I was determined to, once again, prove the "true" intent behind the syndicate's business activities with the prepaid calling card business. Without missing a beat, and with total control of the investigative decisions surrounding the prepaid case, I began an assault that soon was recognized on both camps; that of the "Cosa Nostra" and the law enforcement community. There is an old Italian proverb that is also commonly used in America. The Italian version is as follows: *"Batti il ferro finché è caldo."* The English version, "Strike while the iron is hot." And like the proverb, I did just that.

With their longtime traditional control of extortion and bid-rigging rackets in both New York City and New Jersey, all weakened by years of relentless prosecutions and by regulatory crackdowns, the region's Mafia crime families spearheaded by the Gambino crime family, were switching now to more and more white-collar crimes. I believe that at the time, the mob had a focus primarily on multimillion-dollar frauds in three lucrative businesses: health insurance, prepaid telephone cards, and small Wall Street brokerage houses.

It was unbelievable; they were better organized than in many instances law enforcement, and they understood to adapt to the changes in business practices so they could capitalize on the loopholes, which allowed for the fraud to occur. So, in the mid-'90s, the syndicate got involved with the prepaid calling card business, and within a short period of time, wreaked major damage to the telecommunication industry. They were untouchable, and seeing that their success caused no attention from law enforcement, they continued to loot the poor and the wealthy fat telecommunication industry. They were, in many ways, unstoppable.

But the turning point with the prepaid scheme came on the evening of August 2, 1997, and ended with a major discovery early the next morning. I was listening to an intercepted conversation that occurred on May 28, 1996, and it was between John A. Gotti Junior and his driver, a guy who promoted himself as a carpenter, Anthony Plomitallo. I recall being alone that night working through the voluminous wiretap conversations. It was very late in what essentially became my second job at the White Plains, U.S. Attorney's office. Each day, I would leave the field office located at 7 World Trade around 3 p.m. and head up to the White Plains, Southern District of New York office, to work on the Gotti case. Almost every night I would work until I couldn't keep my eyes open. Well, that particular night, I was sitting there with my headset and tape recorder, intently listening to every word coming out of the mouth of various Mafiosos and their associates. I was about ready to end my nightly ritual when suddenly the conversation turned to just two people, and one was Gotti.

I was unaware at the time of the enormous validity this particular intercepted conversation had to the overall scheme. As I explained earlier, the original OCTF transcript had a great amount of details missing and ultimately, looked nothing like the product I produced after countless reviews and revisions. This is in no way a criticism of the work product produced by others. Those folks, and one that comes to mind, a short, lovely, older woman by the name of Linda who religiously cranked out these transcripts, was amazing. But there was simply too much work on these types of cases and very little to no resources available to perfect the work product. So many of the intercepted conversations, particularly these that discussed fraud, had many gaps in the transcripts. Why? Well, unlike the traditional schemes where both the investigator sitting in the plant and later, the transcriber, had already the necessary experience since the schemes were well documented and quite common, in this scheme, the folks behind the "bug" did not know the scheme that was behind the tele-communication fraud. Therefore, the lack of experience, compiled with being understaffed, resulted in information either missed and/or minimized during the intercept, and later on, the transcripts as well.

Anyway, at one point, as I slowly replayed Gotti's every word, I heard what sounded like the word "bustin'" come out of his mouth. Can this be true? Was Gotti informing Plomitallo that "his" intent with the phone card business was to bust it out? I recall how, after reading repeatedly the newly revised transcript of the conversation, denying my own eyes and ears of what was in front of me, I kept replaying the same few seconds of the conversation where the word "bustin'" was mentioned with the hope to either confirm or deny what appeared to me a major discovery. What was later an even more profound break-through was the fact that Gotti, in that particular conversation, tied the conspiracy events between an earlier prepaid calling card fraud scheme to the one that took place later with his business and Denny McLain, the ex-pitcher for the Detroit Tigers.

A conspiracy to "bust out" the prepaid calling card business that Gotti and the syndicate controlled was intercepted, and I found it! Once I was confident of what was said, I immediately called Echo, who I woke up from a sound sleep. I then did the same to Vince Heintz. I remember excitedly discussing the evidence I heard on the cassette tape, and the next morning, a "buzz" was in the air. Everyone was excited, including the other attorneys from the Southern District of New York.

What I heard in that transcript was a conspiracy being plotted by the head of the Gambino crime family. John "Junior" Gotti, that May 28, 1996, had a conversation where he, for a brief moment, felt he was secure and thus explained to Plomitallo his intent to control an expanding prepaid calling card fraud scheme. That evening, he identified himself as the "master broker" who would control all the prepaid calling card companies. At the time, I was not exactly sure how much influence the Gambino crime family had over this scheme. But after the intercept and as I began to piece together evidence through numerous interviews, strategic search warrants, and listening to every intercepted conversation that followed the May one, it was clear that they had complete control of the distribution of the prepaid calling card market.

It was absolutely amazing, the December 1995 affidavit that was brokered in the judge's kitchen, where simultaneously, I was discussing food with the judge, while Vince Heintz was discussing the merits of the warrant. Those original wiretaps morphed into more and ultimately capturing various criminal enterprises, including the scheme behind the prepaid calling card fraud which was being discussed by the head of the Gambino crime family! The May 28, 1996, conversation, as explained briefly earlier, tied Gotti to the Travel phone card, which had committed major fraud. By the spring of 1996, the Travel Card was activating approximately 20 million phone cards a month before it went bankrupt in late 1996, leaving WorldCom, who, at the time, was the fourth-largest long-distance carrier, with a $94-million debt to cover.

To understand the issue and the reason why Gotti was explaining his plan to have multiple companies up and running had to do with the eventual shutoff of service. The cards sold would eventually not work since the companies producing them had no intention in running a legitimate business or paying the carrier in full. This intercepted conversation explained Gotti's concerns with cards not working, and he provided a solution that would allow the fraud to continue. He explained that by having a card ready to replace the one no longer working, so as to minimize attention and outside scrutiny, would be the new way to proceed.

Thus, the "foundation" of the prepaid calling card investigation had been identified. It was amazing . . . an investigation that started as a preliminary inquiry in 1993 by the United States Senate Subcommittee on Investigations, which requested OCTF's assistance in locating and serving a subpoena upon Leonard Minuto Senior. This was all being driven with the hopes of securing his testimony regarding racketeering in the professional boxing industry. The inquiry identified him as a gambling promoter, a Bronx-based policy gambling operation, and mushroomed in 1994 into a joint Bronx DA and OCTF partnership identifying the organized crime syndicate controlling Minuto. In 1994, I joined the case, and based on my "hunches" that at times seemed like witchcraft, where the hunch turned into reality, overwhelming the industry with subpoenas, conducting physical surveillance at unheard of hours, using the technology of the time by cloning and intercepting pagers communication, and analyzing voluminous phone records that resulted in pen register requests . . . The case moved from a snail's pace to rocket speed.

Echo, who was "the" case agent for OCTF, never misunderstood me. He always encouraged the creativity inside of me to flourish. He was a hobbyist in both writing stories and a singer; thus, creativity was not lacking with Echo. We laughed a bunch, ate great food all the time, but most of all, he enjoyed the close friendship that we had developed between us. In many ways, I was the son he never had, and, in turn, he was almost, in some ways, a father figure to me. This small unique group included Vince and David, who is now with the Secret Service, and thus, his last name will be kept out of the book. Vince would spend countless hours after the normal workday writing extensions and affidavits, and many times, I would join him, which allowed me to ask questions and learn more about the case.

I also learned to understand the way he would approach the evidence collected which I found to be very fascinating. This eagerness, on my part, gave me a very big advantage, and Vince, almost like my very own private tutor, taught me how to intertwine the various criminal activities and thus, think beyond the arrest, or in this case, the criminal act. So within months, I was not only well versed on all the players and their respective roles, but I also understood how to operate in such a sophisticated investigative arena. Not everyone in law enforcement understands such investigations and has the "focus" for this type of work. You are basically living the life that the gangster you are watching is living.

In order to get a full taste of the warrant executed at Nic O Dan Communications, one needs to read the facts as well as the challenges placed forward by the defense. The search warrant was executed on a cool fall day in October 1997, and I was assigned to the credit card squad. ATSAIC Marty Walsh, my boss, agreed to work the warrant in conjunction with Robert Weaver's Squad, which was the New York Electronic Crimes Task Force. This was ideal for me. I was working both credit card investigations and running the Gotti telecommunications investigation, which was technically a case that should have been assigned to Weaver's squad. Again, no one had ever done such an investigation, and prior to me taking it, other agents had reviewed the evidence and wrongfully concluded that there was no case of fraud. By this time, I had retranscribed about 300–400 intercepted wiretapped conversations all on 90 minute, 2-sided cassette tapes. There was indeed major fraud going on!

This tedious, labor-intensive procedure of listening to all the conversations from scratch allowed me to dissect every word recorded, and slowly, I reconstructed the fraud scheme. At this point, the cooperation between the Secret Service and OCTF was at an all-time high, and both Echo and Vince were very pleased with the partnership, and obviously, we were all pleased to work together once again! Soon, I began to utilize the forensic services offered by the Secret Service. For those recorded conversations that were of poor quality, I would transport the original tapes personally down to Washington, D.C., where our forensic services was headquartered. They were fantastic and very amenable to our needs. I would travel almost once a week to D.C. to our forensic lab to enhance audio sound on the intercepted conversations. No one ever questioned it, and it was done moments after a phone call was made for the need to do so. It was on one of these flights I actually ended up sitting next to Mark Pomaranz. At the time, he was still in private practice and not the head of the criminal division for SDNY. That came approximately 2 years later during plea negotiations.

Anyway, soon after the search warrant and the transfer of Marty to the Long Island Secret Service office, I was unofficially transferred to Weaver's Electronic Crimes Task Force. Bob Weaver, who became both a good friend and mentor, did not want to see this case go down the drain, and the new Special Agent in Charge, Chip Smith, was in agreement. The new boss that replaced Marty in the credit card squad, who will remain unnamed, other than using his first name Steve, was a complete clown; *palacio* in Italian. He was transferred up from Washington, D.C., and a complete zero. He was my official immediate supervisor, and he quickly pissed off Echo and soon afterward, Vince, with his out-of-place comments regarding how to run the case and who should be interviewed. The guy was honestly completely in over his head with regards to the investigation, and above all, wore a pinky ring pretending he knew best. What bothered me then and still does today was his lack of humility. It was obvious at this point to me, to Echo, and to Vince, the Secret Service, although an aggressive agency with regards to arresting and making low-level cases, was completely out of its league with this one. Anyway, I had prepared for the warrant, and this search was going to be my "reintroduction" to the Gottis and to the case.

My official title had now changed from Detective Investigator Pasquale Perrotta to now Special Agent Nino Perrotta. This switch one day placed Gotti Junior through a loop. The story will follow, but let me share the events that took place on October 7, 1997. A warrant was executed at Nic O Dan Communications located in Queens, New York. We had our search team and our evidence photographer, Joe Chow, who was an Asian man, no more than 4 foot 7 and quite funny. The search team was comprised of several agents from the Secret Service as well as OCTF investigators, such as my mentor Echo Guadioso and analyst Marie Boss. On the Service side, we had Marty Walsh, my boss, Robert "Bob" Weaver, who would be my new boss, and Jack Shaughnessy who was the backup, the No. 2 in the Electronic Crime Task Force. Shaughnessy was an "agent's agent" and someone who you could trust on all fronts. Like Marty and Bob, Jack supported me and had trust in my decision making, so never once did he present a speed bump to any of my requests. A former PPD guy, Jack and Bob loved the hard-charging attitude I brought to the squad.

Anyway, before we hit the place, we did our homework and knew that adjacent to Nic O Dan Communication was Carmine Agnello's business, Jamaica Auto Salvage. Carmine at the time was married to Victoria Gotti, John's sister. They have since divorced, but he was a complete nut job and one scary-looking mobster. I'll never forget that soon after the search warrant was executed, Carmine came outside the premises and was ranting and raving, basically his normal demeanor, and from nowhere, Joe Chow, like a cat, sprang out and landed by Carmine's side, instantly slapping him on his stomach, and in his thick Asian accent said, "You, you, big tummy man, you like hamburga. Ha! Ha! Ha!" Carmine, a bit startled, immediately turned bright red, looked up and over to Steve Dobies, who was a giant in size, and said, "Who the fuck is that?" Dobies, who was equally confused and a bit slow, responded with a simple motion shrugging his shoulders. After the Chow incident, nothing came out of Carmine's mouth for the rest of the day, and he basically disappeared back into his office.

While we continued with the search, tucked away in a corner of a room neatly organized were the intercepted cassette recordings provided to the defense team of the imprisoned John Gotti. These were obviously intended for the defense team, which was tasked to unravel the infamous FBI case where Sammy "The Bull" Gravano became a cooperating witness against the Gambinos. I couldn't help but notice that the recorded conversations all labeled cassette tapes were no more than a third of what we intercepted on the current targets, including Gotti Senior's son.

When we got to "Junior" Gotti's office, Shaughnessy noticed several pictures and statutes of American Indians and had a puzzled look on his face. It was not until later that we were informed that "Junior" had a thing for the American Indians and believed that the Gotti family, like the American Indians, were persecuted, and that both he and his sister would later say during various meetings that their family, the Gotti family, were like the American Indians, constantly hunted down and persecuted, and thus, they believed, but John especially, that they were "the last of the Mohicans."

A hulking man who identified himself as Steve Dobies was at the entrance to Nic O Dan. I looked up at him and, without a word, showed him the search warrant. We have major case squad NYPD there as well for support and backup if needed. Steve had to stand around 6 foot 3 and had a lurking-type look. He was standing there and shortly after, we told him to move out of the way and stay outside so we can conduct our search. After a brief moment, he came back with one of the Secret Service agents, John Toal. Steve had a concerned look on his face and informed me that his boss, John Gotti Junior, was on the cell and wanted to speak to me, and that it was urgent. I took the call on Steve's cell phone, and in a very cordial manner, "Junior" explained that there was absolutely no need for such an event.

If I had asked in advance, he would have been more than happy to cooperate and make copies of business files, and in the same breath, offered me and the search team some espresso and pastries. I smirked since I understood the friendly gesture but respectfully declined, thanked him, and handed the phone back to Dobies and went on with the search. In the end, we got what we were looking for and left. At this time, the only interaction I had with Gotti was on surveillance. At no other time did I speak with him, and the feeling was a bit overwhelming. I loved the hunt as well as conducting the investigation.

The fact that I spoke to my "target" was an absolute charge that is best understood by the few who have taken on a big challenge or risk. The feeling was amazing! I could feel my blood flowing through my body, and I recalled being very calm and focused, which made me ever so confident of my surroundings and purpose. It was a feeling that came only on rare occasions, but I honestly lived for it.

The search was important. It provided that the "conspiracy" conversation we heard in the car moved forward, and intent was established. The search warrant also produced very interesting information, an unusual amount of phone cards ordered for print, and thousands of labels with an 800 number followed with an activation pin. Our forensics experts determined that the number of cards activated for use did not match with the amount of prepaid calling cards printed, and they did not correlate with the new 800 number/activation label. In addition to the prepaid calling cards, which were called Liberty Tel, we found a document on the secretary's computer. This document seemed to read like a diary that contained a history of events that involved the prepaid calling card business and several key individuals.

At the time, I was unsure what exactly this document meant, but as I moved forward with the case and developed it, it was clear that the search warrant was an even bigger success than anticipated. In addition to the evidence that provided great data, we had industry experts like Meric Bloch who provided invaluable guidance. So it made perfect sense that the legal defense team contended that the October 7, 1997, warrant was unconstitutionally overbroad, and they essentially attempted to argue that by providing no "readily" ascertainable guidelines as to what items were to be seized, it essentially authorized a general search of the premises.

The federal search warrant read:

YOU ARE HEREBY AUTHORIZED to enter [97-11 Sutphin Boulevard], and to conduct a search thereof and of any person found therein, and to search any container found in such location or on such person wherein any of the property described below may be found; and to seize any such property if found in that location and/or on such person, as follows: (1) property used to commit certain crimes, to wit: Grand Larceny, in violation of Article 155 of the New York State Penal Law; Scheme to Defraud in the First Degree, in violation of section 190.65 of the New York State Penal Law; violations of sections 1804 and 1805 of the New York State Tax Law (relating to the filing of false personal and corporate income tax returns); and violations of sections 1810 of the New York State Tax Law (relating to the failure to pay personal and corporate income tax); (2) property evidencing the commission of those crimes; and (3) property identifying, and tending to identify, the persons who have committed those crimes, and who have been victimized by the commission of those crimes; all such property consisting of the following business and financial records, to the extent that such were produced between April 1996 and the present: A. Documents related to business transactions in which Nic O Dan Telecommunications, and/or John A. Gotti, and/or Anthony Plomitallo, and/or Steven Dobies, and/or Delmy Avila, and/or Michael Zambouros, have engaged, as well as all contracts to which Nic O Dodan Telecommunications, and/or John A. Gotti, and/or Anthony Plomitallo, and/or Steven Dobies, and/or Delmy Avila, and/or Michael Zambouros, have been parties, or in connection with which Nic O Dan Telecommunications, and/or John A. Gotti, and/or Anthony

Plomitallo, and/or Steven Dobies, and/or Delmy Avila, and/ or Michael Zambouros, have transacted business, all such transactions and/or contracts relating to the marketing of telephone service access codes, specifically toll-free (or "1[800]" or "1[888]" numbers) and personal identification numbers (or "PINS"), under any of the following brands of pre-paid calling cards and/or involving any of the following firms or persons: Q-Card, MVP Card, Liberty Card, Travel Card, and any other prepaid calling cards found [in 97-11 Sutphin Boulevard], AT&T, SPRINT, MCI, Tel-Central Communications, H.G. Telecom, Inc., Universal Communications Network, Inc. ("UCN"), Atlas Communications, SMS Q-Card, Inc., Frank Cali, Vincent Annunziata, Salvatore Scala, Michael DiGiorgio, Steven Chaplain, Anthony Amorous; all such documents to consist of contracts, subcontracts, purchase orders, invoices, and receipts for payment, as well as memoranda of communications between and/or among any of the aforesaid firms and/or persons; B. Property evidencing the quantities and monetary values of telephone service access codes marketed under the brand names Q-Card, MVP Card, and Liberty Card, as well as any other prepaid calling cards found in [97-11 Sutphin Boulevard], and evidencing the identities of actual access codes marketed through any of these brand names, such property to include actual pre-paid calling cards bearing these brand names, as well as contracts, subcontracts, purchase orders, invoices, receipts for payment, and related memoranda, as pertinent to the marketing of telephone calling services through the distribution of access codes under such brand names, and as pertinent to the manufacturing and printing of such brand names, and as pertinent to the distribution of such brand-name cards; C. Telephone directories and other memoranda containing the names, addresses,

telephone numbers, pager numbers, and other data reflect-
ing the identities of the persons and firms enumerated in
paragraph A, above; D. Records of the proceeds generat-
ed by the distribution of the above-named pre-paid calling
cards brands, including the financial records of Nic O Dan
Telecommunications, and any other firms or persons if such
records reflect the generation of income by the distribution
of the pre-paid calling card brands named in paragraph A,
above, as follows: cash receipts and disbursements journals;
bank statements; records of check deposits and disburse-
ments; account reconciliations; canceled checks; check
stubs; and check registers; for all operating, expense and
payroll accounts of Nic O Dan Telecommunications, and/or
other firms engaged in the distribution of the above-named
pre-paid calling card brands; E. Records containing informa-
tion related to Nic O Dan Telecommunication's liability for
and payment of corporate income tax (including documents
of the type listed in paragraph D, above), and related to Nic
O Dan Telecommunication's payment of income, in the forms
of salaries, commissions, bonuses, and loans to John A. Gotti,
as follows: payroll records; bank statements; records of cash
and check deposits and disbursements; account reconcilia-
tions; canceled checks; check stubs; check registers; W-2
forms; 1099 forms; W-4 forms; federal payroll forms 940 and
941; Gotti's individual and Nic O Dan's corporate income tax
returns; and withholding schedules.

Roadblocks, both bureaucratic and personally motivated, were slowly and continuously placed in our way, and they began to increase,
some even coming from within the Secret Service. As the pinky ring
supervisor became more and more embolden with his nonsense,
he began to slowly attempt to influence investigative decisions. The

confidence level started with the "deer in a headlight look" as he sat down in my cubicle soon after he had replaced Marty Walsh. As a new ATSAIC, he was full of himself and had an air of arrogance that was sad to witness and frustrating and demoralizing to experience. I recall his conversation that first day we meet. I was in my cubicle, and he grabbed the vacant seat across from me. "So, I understand you got a real good one here, huh?"

I looked up and without making eye contact responded with a quick, smart-ass response. "Yeah, she's from Long Island" knowing that he was referring to the case. I quickly put him off guard. There was a picture of a tall blonde on my desk; they changed so frequently that folks in the squad made jokes about it. He responded by saying, "No, I mean the Gotti case, so tell me about it." So I begin briefing and within 10 minutes I saw the blank stare in his eyes and realized he was completely lost. Almost instantly, the case that was basically scheduled and planned strategically between Vince and Echo and I turned into a circus act where I was now just becoming a part of the backstage help, and the new boss was the circus ringmaster calling the shots—shots that made absolutely no sense whatsoever.

So there was a conscious effort by the three of us to minimize his involvement. It took Echo no time at all to call this guy a wannabe, and Vince grew tired of the educational courses he needed to give him literally during every meeting. Vince did his best to not confuse the poor dumb bastard while he tried to desperately catch up. This was not the type of case one could just wing it. You needed to absorb the facts, and as a supervisor, make sure the case agent was abiding by the criminal procedure code and ultimately, respect his investigative opinion. It was time for a change; otherwise, this would all end up being a waste of time.

With the drastic "management" change now set in stone, I continued to forge ahead. We located and interviewed Denny McLain's unnamed family member and soon afterward, made a bold attempt at flipping "Eli". In between those two interviews, I was still managing a normal caseload, as well as participating in the office rotation for protection. The workload was overwhelming, and although never complaining about it, I internalized the stress and dealt with it. Heck, now that I was knee-deep in the case again, what choice did I really have?

I worked very hard night and day, but due to the office politics being created by the new ATSAIC, the Gotti case was slowly fumbling along, and it seemed that the "zoom"; a nick name Echo gave me, which basically expressed my "fast-paced" momentum towards everything I did but in particular the case, had now slowed down to an almost a halt. I recall specifically the interview on December 23, 1997, of the target Eli "M." The guy was contacted by phone by me one day and he, already knowing who I was and the overwhelming impact I was having on "business," preferred to meet me late one evening at our office. So voluntarily, Eli agreed to meet me at 7 WTC.

Eli came alone, no attorney, no goons, and although he had provided excellent indictable information during the interview, Vince and I agreed to not have him arrested. Rather, allow Eli to conclude on his own that he was somewhat of a cooperating witness and had fooled us all. Of course, as expected that evening, while Eli waited in the interview room, I was met with resistance from the pinky ring-wearing supervisor. He expressed very adamantly, while pointing his finger at me, that arresting Malouf now would be the better way to go and wanted that to happen. After an intense period of discussion, where I luckily had Vince present, "his" idea was eventually squashed. It did not matter that we had all agreed prior as the initial plan. The knucklehead supervisor had an "epiphany" and now wanted to do things his way—and always at a cost to others.

So with Vince providing both "cover and concealment," I was able to get most of my investigative ideas pushed through my bosses without much interference. I also had moral support from Bob Weaver who would report to senior management what this "mameluke" was doing, and basically, they kept him accountable, for the most part. The guy left me alone whenever there was real work to be done, which was absolutely fine with me. His backup, Special Agent John Buechele , on the other hand, was absolutely great and helped me extensively, whenever possible. John, who sat through numerous interviews and dealt with the ATSAIC's insecurities, never once complained to me. It was only when this particular supervisor thought he could person-ally benefit, did he replace John and insert himself. This occurred on January 21, 1998, the day both the Secret Service and OCTF coordi-nated and planned the arrests on the case. The primary federal arrest agency, the United States Secret Service, led the arrest teams. Other agencies, including the FBI, NYPD, and IRS, were also participants in the 30-plus simultaneous arrests of both members and associates of the Gambino crime family. On that day, John Gotti Junior was also arrested, and although the event was not particularly an exciting one for Echo or me, it was definitely for those seeking "instant glory," and that day was called "Operation Ricochet."

9

The Bottom of the Last Inning and Here Comes Operation Ricochet!

It was late November of 1997, and after speaking to Denny McLain on numerous occasions at the United States Attorney's Office for the Southern District of New York, located in White Plains, New York, it was clear that he was going to be a "major player" in another game: the blame game. From the onset, McLain used every excuse in the book and blamed all the mishaps that occurred in his life, including his business activities at Tel Central Communications, on others. Denny had an excuse for absolutely everything that went wrong in his life, including his most recent fraud scheme. This guy wanted to claim that MCI had overcharged his account, and due to a loophole that he believed had legitimacy, he was going around telling everyone that his debt with MCI was going to be erased. It was unbelievable to me how this man saw everything as someone else's problem.

What I found amazing was that Denny never took ownership for his actions and refused responsibility for anything. Between the constant requests for Diet Pepsi, fried chicken, and pastries, it became very clear that he was going to play us to the very end. Regardless, Denny wasn't going anywhere since he was serving time for defrauding a pension fund and was serving time he, of course, blamed others for. After a painful attempt to get him to confess to the scheme, we moved past him and brought in a close family member who was directly involved with Denny. To protect him we will call this person Lou.-

With Lou, it was another story. He was a nervous individual, and in my opinion, basically a good man who got caught up with the larger-than-life personality of his father-in-law, the former great major-league ball player. During that December 19, 1997, interview, Lou laid out the groundwork as to how his father-in-law would create constant opportunities to defraud consumers of their phone time whenever they utilized their prepaid phone cards. The act was simple in scope. It basically involved shutting the users' usage of their purchased prepaid calling cards. It was that plain and simple. So while the poor unsuspecting consumer, many of whom were hardworking, lower-income individuals, were speaking to family overseas, Denny, from the comfort of his own home or office, monitoring this activity from his computer, would shut a series of phone cards off, forcing the consumer to reconnect and automatically deducting a fee, typically $1 from the card for that connection to occur.

This was called a "bong" charge, and now Lou confirmed that this was an act that Denny was known to do. He continued by explaining the below-market pricing and the affects that had on the switches that handled the phone traffic. Folks would receive a busy signal whenever they tried to use the cards. This was the direct result of extremely attractive below-market rates which caused a huge demand on the market. There was absolutely no-to-minimal investment made in the infrastructure (the switches) coupled with the creation of enough of a

"blame game" to muddy the waters. It was, in fact, an almost unde-
tectable scheme.

The ring of thieves that collectively participated in committing this
fraud had, in my opinion, done a great job at layering the scheme in
such a manner that it was both complex and offered many opportunities for an investigator to come up on dead ends and convoluted
leads. Lou, however, was able to lay out the process, explain, and
most importantly, verify, what I already knew; how certain cards were
replaced by others. Lou was instrumental. He was a witness with an
inside view of the crime.

Lou offered specific information and explained how the rates offered
by Denny were completely below the market rate and how there
was absolutely no way he would be able to pay MCI for the minutes
purchased. The offering of below-market prices was a technique to
attract consumers and rapidly capture the marketplace. Denny knew
fully well what he was doing and was instructed to place certain
cards on his switch. The Mafia had control of which cards would be
distributed and sold in the market. This was captured in the May 28,
1996, intercepted conversation where Gotti explained "the process"
to Plomitallo.

Lou then talked about his experience with the Mafia. He stated that
one day both he and Denny met with a group in New Jersey, sometime in late 1996, to discuss business and an IPO. This meeting had
several Mafia figures, like Gene Lombardo and a "known" crook
that specialized in fraudulent IPOs. At one point after the meeting,
they headed to a bar, and there, an individual who's name has been
changed "Michael"" asked Lou a very important question. Would he

take over the business in the event Denny had to go to jail? A question Lou explained that he was not sure if he should provide an answer. He explained that he was intimidated and afraid at that point that both he and Denny may not come out of the meeting alive.

The operation's briefing leading up to the arrests were held at 7 World Trade Center. There, we had all the respective leadership to discuss the arrest operation, protocol, and safety measures. John Buechele was handling the operations order and the coordination of the briefing while I continued to work on the case. I never stopped working the investigation. I knew that this was going to be one of those cases where we would most definitely have to go to trial, so I wanted to be prepared as much as possible for when the time came. I was prepared and ready. The rumblings had started; we had the FBI complaining that the Secret Service was given permission to affect all of the arrests as opposed to selecting them. In addition to the arrests, there were all sorts of issues being raised on how to handle John Gotti Junior on game day. It all seemed a bit petty and irrelevant to me. I mean, the guy was aware that his arrest was imminent due to the local city newspaper articles printed about it on a weekly basis.

I recall being dispatched to affect the arrest of Junior with Bronx D.A. Detective Sgt. Investigator Frank Thorpe. We were in Oyster Bay, Long Island, and it was a cold morning. Out in front of Junior's home camped out with their TV cameras and lights were the press. Of course, Junior was not there, but we needed to confirm it. It was funny . . . The FBI had requested SWAT teams for these arrests and wanted to make a production out of arresting Gotti Junior. Echo would not have any part of it. I believe he did everything he could to undermine their production. At the time, he kept his plans to himself, but not until recently did he share his plans with me.

Thorpe and I were tasked to go to Gotti's Oyster Bay residence and see if Junior was there. Echo made it clear from the start that he did not want this to be a circus and seeing that the FBI wanted to make it such, he called Richard Rehbock. Echo requested that Rehbock have John surrender at a location that made sense to everyone. Later, when Rehbock called Echo back, Bill from the FBI overhead the conversation Echo was having and reported back to Jack that Echo was speaking to Gotti's lawyer. Word about the conversation got back to Vince Heintz, and although it was completely distorted and one-sided, nevertheless, it threw Vince into such a frenzy that he immediately went to Mitch Lambert, Echo's boss at the time, and asked for him to be fired.

Why was Echo so upset and determined to get this arrest of John Gotti "Junior" over with? The main reason was that Echo, a seasoned investigator with a "keen sense" of smelling bullshit from a mile away had it up to his ears with the FBI. Despite my own experience of nonsense with the FBI, Echo lived it throughout almost the entire Gambino investigation. Soon after the OCTF bugs were up and the investigators began listening to Greg DePlama's rants and raves, it was clear from DePalma's conversations that an unified FBI agent was communicating facts about OCTF's case to a local shop keeper in Westchester County. In an effort to maintain the integrity of certain privileged and confidential information, I will keep things vague. Echo, Vince and OCTF senior management wanted to do the right thing by sharing information with the Bureau. The result of this good will? Well it was exactly what the FBI has been known to do. The FBI, was invited by OCTF to participate in search warrant activities. This good faith effort by OCTF was repaid as revealed later in the investigation by the FBI withholding information about certain aspects of the case. According to Echo, his frustration with the FBI grew due to their lack of partnership, information sharing and subtle attempts to take over the case.

Well, I guess there was reason to send me and Thorpe to the residence because of the fact that when we got there, due to the way we were dressed and looked, the news reporters did not give us a second glance. They never suspected we were the feds and assumed we were part of the wise guys who were in the backdrop. I was clean-shaven, wore a dark suit under a long black overcoat. There was nothing on me that depicted law enforcement and Thorpe was dressed the same, although he remained in the car. I walked up to the gate and spoke to the caretaker who spoke Italian and asked him if *"il padrone era a casa."* He responded back in Italian, "No, the owner is not home," and on that note, I signaled with a nod my satisfaction, turned, and walked back to the car.

The press pretended I didn't exist partly because they assumed I was a gangster and why would anyone want to get in the way of a gangster. Well, that was until I opened the car door and in plain view was a police light visible for all to see. Someone yelled out, "Oh shit, they're cops." Within seconds, the lights and the cameras turned on. I had just enough time to enter the vehicle, lock the door so my partner, Thorpe, could put the car in reverse, and get out of the area.

I eventually connected with Echo, and as we were heading back to the Armory, we were both waiting and sitting in the back of an unmarked police vehicle when Echo received a call from Vince. Echo turned to me and explained that Richard Rehbock, John's attorney, was coordinating the surrender through the U.S. Attorney's Office. When the call came, Echo had offered me the honor of handcuffing Gotti Junior, a major compliment to me. However, this was not to happen. We learned minutes later that Jack and my boss with the pinky ring had Gotti Junior secured and they were transporting him to the Armory. The two were caught bringing Gotti into processing and the press photographed the three entering the building. My boss who was wearing a raid jacket would brag about his arrest in the years that followed. Years later, he recounted his exploits to the counterfeit squad while telling tall tales, when an agent stood up and for the record said, "Hey, you didn't arrest Gotti; that was Nino's case."

The arrest of Gotti Junior and the successful investigation into his crew was one outcome I am very proud of. We beat the FBI at their own game. Now the FBI volunteered fingerprint technicians for the arrest day, and, of course, no one saw any issue with using the technicians. What was agreed upon during the planning stages of Operation Ricochet was a simultaneous arrest of 45 members/associates of the Gambino crime family. The agreed terms between the OCTF and Secret Service were for the lead arresting agency to be the Secret Service. Well, the FBI technicians, I quickly realized that day, had in their possession FBI fingerprint cards with the ROI number identifying the arresting agency as the FBI. So for every damn "perp" that was walked in that day, no matter what the charge was, credit would go to and the arrest would be considered an FBI arrest.

They really were good at this and credit be given when due, even if it was an underhanded move. So what I did to counter this strategic win was that I printed Gotti myself on Secret Service fingerprint cards. This would ensure that when the arrest charges made it through the system, the credit went to the United States Secret Service and not the FBI. Yes, a small victory, but it did rob them of their scheme. Top brass of the Secret Service and OCTF were involved in the entire arrest planning.

Thinking back I joined the investigation back in 1994–1995 time frame, listening to Craig DePalma ranting and raving in his home. For a brief time while I was there, the investigation did have Craig's phone tapped, but it was believed that he was not relevant and therefore, the court order to listen in on his cell phone was not renewed. Pre-Secret Service involvement in the case that got me both in the spotlight as well as in hot water, was the fact that I went back and listened to those recorded conversations and found evidence of criminality when Craig was on the cell phone. I convinced Vince to go back up on Craig's cell phone.

There was a great deal going on with Craig that was basically missed during the previous investigation. Although he was not as vocal as his dad Greg, he was communicating with Gotti Junior. This was enough. Part of our ability to target Gotti Junior was the information obtained from these cell phone conversations, surveillance that was conducted from those communications, as well as from his cloned beeper which provided the team with real-time transmittals. I fine-tuned my investigative skills prior to joining the Secret Service and increased confidence in my own ability. These two factors helped me tremendously when I returned to the case.

Vincent Heintz was on his way to work, and from the corner of his eye, he noticed Craig DePalma near the White Plains Courthouse, obviously leaving his weekly meeting there and heading in a direction that did not take him directly home. Vince was a cop at heart and a National Guard Infantry Officer; his instincts were rarely wrong. He and I were very close and spoke constantly about the case. We would spend hours every day simply discussing strategy and rehashing every aspect of the investigation. So when he called me, I knew it was important. Craig was on house detention and could only travel under specific guidelines that were prearranged during his arrest. He, at the time, had to go home and not deviate his travel route from his home to the Federal Courthouse in White Plains. Vince, knowing something was amiss, initiated surveillance, and at the time, I did not know that he had called the FBI to assist, and they declined due to not having enough advance notice. They were unable to execute.

So Vince calls me; I'm in my office at 7 World Trade Center, and he's in White Plains. Under normal conditions with no traffic, one would need at least 45 minutes to an hour to get there. Vince explained the situation, and as soon as he was done talking to me, I called upon a loyal agent who was a true investigator, my friend Michael. He was assigned to the Secret Service White Plains Office, an office of about seven people, including a boss. Michael, in his office doing paper-work, immediately grabbed his gun and jacket and headed out to join Vince on the impromptu surveillance. Vince was on the tail; Michael was about to meet him; and I got into my blacked out 1997 Firebird with its full police light package, a rarity in those days. I bolted out of the garage and within minutes was on the Henry Hudson Parkway heading northbound.

I went as fast as possible, lights and sirens all the way and with little traffic, thankfully, I made it within 20–25 minutes. He relieved Vince who headed to the office and upon my direction began to prepare a subpoena. As I approached the scene, I noticed they were in Denny's restaurant, with Michael having entered inside, ordered some ham and eggs of some sort and watched as Craig met with some associates. Immediately, I knew from my investigative experience that the restaurant had live video surveillance recordings for security purposes. I would need this footage to provide teeth to the field report that I was going to prepare later that evening.

Craig was meeting with folks from the construction industry, and we found out later it was to resolve a beef, and he thought no one was watching . . . While they were sitting there, I walked into the restaurant unnoticed and with a quick flash of my Secret Service gold badge, I informed the manager that I would need his recorded video surveillance and that a subpoena would be provided shortly. He immediately complied and assured me that the surveillance video would be provided as soon as the subpoena was delivered. I thanked him and returned to my vehicle. Craig was in violation of his court-ordered detention and for this, he would soon realize how painful this maneuver would be to the Gambino crime family.

Now please note that if this had happened 2 or 3 days prior, I would have been unable to participate because I was working a protection assignment. The life of a Secret Service agent was that volatile and the dual rolls we held were a challenge. Although Michael was great, he did not have the institutional knowledge of the case necessary to make decisions based on incoming information that changed rapidly. Surveillance from the restaurant led us to Craig's girlfriend's home where he had approved house detention—an apartment in Bronxville area, Westchester County. His girlfriend was a real looker, a stripper who was into rough sex I learned that day.

As Craig pulled into the underground garage of the apartment complex and once I received a green light from Vince who was now at the U.S. Attorney's Office, I quickly hit the lights and siren. I "lit him up," as they say, and he stopped his car. I got out of the car, introduced myself, and explained that he was in violation of his home detention. Mike was there supporting me and making sure that we had no safety issues. Craig whined, and I gave him no opportunity but to tell him to park the car and "Let's go upstairs." Now with home detention, he has no right to privacy, and since that was the case, I began to search his home. My partner was there and providing entry security since we did not want any problems or distractions.

While searching his apartment, I feigned a need to make an urgent business call. Normally, I would have used the house phone, but instead, I pulled out my Motorola flip phone. The real reason for this maneuver was to see how Craig made and received calls so as to keep him in communication with his superiors within the Gambino crime family. I soon realized that inside the apartment cell coverage was weak to nonexistent in certain areas. I made a statement to no one in particular but in a loud voice about "the fucking poor reception in this place" and being unable to make a cell call. I looked at Mike and offered a small but noticeable smile, letting him know I had a plan. I couldn't believe it. Craig responded from the couch with "Go to the kitchen and lean out the window. That's where I get the best reception."

At that point I knew cell phones were being used between Craig and his associates. Within a few minutes of him making that statement, during the search, I located a cell phone in the kitchen, which was inoperable but well hidden behind some dishes. Now, shortly after the incident, the girlfriend arrived and did nothing but scream, curse, and complain about the feds always harassing her boyfriend. She entered the bathroom, and then attempted to leave the apartment, BUT not without a search of her purse. During the search, I find the cell phone "he" was using, and, of course, we were able to prove this with the call records. Oh, and during my subsequent interview of the girlfriend, it all came full circle, as she was unable to explain away or tell me to whom those phone calls were made.

Once I got to the bedroom, the exciting stuff began. I found about 20k in cash, another violation, and chains and photos of him, the girlfriend, and a black male in some of the most sadistic sexual acts I had before or since seen. I did Craig a favor and handed him $1,000 from the money he had hidden. I also gave him the sick photos but vouchered the chains and whips for further investigative follow-up. The Gambino crime family had gotten another taste of the Secret Service, and I can tell you they were not accustomed to such aggressiveness.

By the end of 1998, the "core" team comprised of Vince, Vinney, Davie, Echo and myself, investigating the Gambino crime family had grown but the original members had mastered the art of investigating long-term investigations. We were now second to none, and our expertise made us subject matter experts to the point that whenever a voice was heard over an intercepted conversation, the name of who was speaking and whom he was associated with would be made available from memory in a matter of a few seconds. At that time, we were considered, among our peers, as a modern-day version of the movie *The Untouchables*. It seemed all was going well . . . until the investigative team received a series of blows that required our attention.

10

A Full Count & the Phone Card Charges Are Dropped

Reflecting now, it seemed that the urgency from the prosecution team to get a plea deal had overshadowed the goal of serving justice. One could argue that by having the phone card investigation part of the overall indictment, it forced the Gambino crime family to accept a plea. One would also argue how could this be? Well, for starters as later explained, if convicted of a fraud such as what the phone card case would have been, the Gambino's, Gotti would have had to pay restitution. So of course this needed be removed from the case the mob was not in the business in returning hard earned money that was "cleverly" stolen. In any event, it was a blow to the hard work and dedication the Secret Service had committed to the investigation, but at the time, it was the smartest move for me to agree to folding the phone card case and agree to a global plea deal that excluded the fraud perpetrated against the poor folks using the phone cards and the telecommunication industry.

Federal prosecutors yesterday dropped phone-card-scam charges from a massive racketeering indictment against John

A. "Junior" Gotti. But prosecutors said the action would have no effect on the remaining charges accusing Gotti of running the Gambino crime family, extorting money from the topless club Scores, and robbing a drug dealer at gunpoint. His trial is set to begin early next month. Junior, who the feds say has been running his Dapper Dad's mob interests while the elder Gotti serves a life term in prison, called yesterday's action a victory. "I was a victim. I lost a lot of money on that deal," Junior told The Post *in federal court in White Plains. Gotti had been charged along with three others, including former Cy Young Award-winning pitcher Denny McLain, with selling bogus, prepaid phone cards that soaked consumers for millions.*

But that aspect of the case began to fall apart when federal investigators started looking into phone-card fraud allegations against at least one large telecommunications company — and it appeared that Junior himself may have been the victim of a rip-off. The charges were not dropped against McLain and two others. **"FEDS DROP PHONE RAP FROM GOTTI INDICTMENT";** *New York Post* **Article; by Al Guart, March 12, 1999**

Organized crime is muscling into the telecommunications industry, plundering millions of dollars from industry giants and picking the pockets of consumers. Mob-linked firms including one controlled by John (Junior) Gotti have made big scores with pre-paid phone cards, court papers, and law enforcement sources say. The alleged scams are being investigated by two federal grand juries. The phone-card industry is ripe for corruption, having mushroomed to an estimated $2 billion last year from $40 million in 1993, authorities say. "It's better than drugs, because they're making so much money and the penalties are zip," a veteran organized crime investigator said. Phone cards enable callers to buy local or long-distance time in denominations ranging from $5 to $100.

They are distributed by firms that have purchased access to phone systems like WorldCom and MCI. The cards are widely available in convenience stores, newsstands, and other outlets. They are particularly popular with students and in immigrant communities because they often offer cheap rates for calls to specific countries. In a typical scam, a phone-card firm contracts with a long-distance provider, sells thousands of cards to consumers, then doesn't pay the phone system, which, in turn, deactivates the customers' cards. One company Communications Network Corp. (Conetco) began selling phone cards in the summer of 1995, and by spring of 1996, it was activating $20 million worth of cards a month.

When it went bankrupt late in 1996, it left WorldCom, the nation's No. 4 long-distance carrier, holding the bag for $94 million. A Brooklyn federal grand jury is investigating the alleged fraud. Sources say the firm was a front for the Gambino crime family now headed by Gotti. Other reputed Gambino mobsters tied to the firm include Joseph (Joe the German) Watts and John (Jackie the Nose) D'Amico, sources say. Watts, who pleaded guilty in 1996 to disposing of a body in connection with a Gambino family slaying, allegedly is a mob trailblazer in phone scams. Watts' lawyer, James LaRossa, acknowledged that his client worked for Conetco as a sales agent. But LaRossa said any fraud occurred after his client went to jail in 1996. "From every bit of information I have, his involvement was completely legitimate, and the company was running appropriately," LaRossa said. "And if there were *thefts, they were after he left." Watts was paid $668,000 in commissions including $395,000 after he was imprisoned, court records show. Bankruptcy papers say $45 million in Conetco funds are missing. When the firm shut down, more than a thousand small merchants and untold numbers of consumers were left with cards that didn't work. "We lost $200; for us that's a lot of money," said Mohamed Saker, a Brooklyn man who owns a newsstand at the Rockaway Parkway subway stop on the L line, and retailed Conetco's cards. "The guy that sold it to us disappeared."*

An unrelated federal grand jury in White Plains is hearing evidence about Gotti's phone-card company as part of a broader probe into the alleged mobster and the construction industry. Gotti's lawyer, Richard Rehbock, said his client has committed no crimes. He said authorities "have interfered incredibly with his legitimate pursuits," and claimed Gotti's firm lost money because investigators seized 13,000 phone cards. "They would like very much to throw a marquee name into an indictment," Rehbock said. Gotti's card company, formed in the spring of 1996 and no longer operating, was called Nic O Dan Communications and was run by his one-time driver, Anthony Plomitallo.

A source said Gotti's company took MCI and two other long-distance carriers for more than $50 million in a scam in which they ran up bills and sold discounted cards before they were shut down. The state Organized Crime Task Force and the Secret Service raided the firm in February and again in October, seizing business records, computers, and thousands of Liberty Tel cards, which have the Statue of Liberty emblazoned on their faces. Secret Service agents also executed a *search warrant in November at a Florida company that manu-factured the cards for Gotti's firm. That company, Ameriplast, is not a target of the probe. Court papers said investigators were seeking any documents or business records linked to Liberty Tel, Gotti, Plomitallo, or a number of other people and companies. An official at Ameriplast said 26 agents spent nine or 10 hours at his company and went through its computer-ized record system.* **"MOB DIALS UP PHONE CARDS"; *New York Daily News*, William Rashbaum, January 11, 1998**

These two articles in New York City's most favored newspapers tell a tale of two cities. They represent the highs and lows of this inves-tigation and represent a whole lot more than just the words used to convey what happened. I realized to my great disdain that all of the hard work and dedication placed into identifying the scheme, and then collecting the necessary evidence was now going to be dropped from the plea negotiations.

It is painful whenever I read the articles written about how charges on the case were dropped. No matter how many times I have read the press coverage over the years since the investigation, I remain angry over the information presented to the public. The very article which was written approximately a year earlier, written by another reporter, lays out the scheme and mentions several members of the syndicate, including Gotti Junior, as key players. This was not a one-time fraud. It was an attack by the Mafia on an industry that had its own issues, but regardless, the fraud I identified was specific and in the end was quite simple to prove. Why then were the charges against the head of the Gambino crime family dropped?

I believe the charges were dropped because John Gotti Junior, when negotiating his plea deal, wanted nothing to do with restitution. If convicted or if he took a plea, the amount he would need to pay in restitution would be staggering. In the syndicate, money and the loss of it weighs supreme over all other options. Mobsters look at doing time in prison as part of doing business; it is a cost they are willing to pay.

Think about it . . . With only one great scheme, if caught, you negotiate with law enforcement and within a decade or less in prison, there will be a pot of gold waiting for you. Now, not only were the charges dropped against Gotti Junior, but against Denny McLain, and the other defendants, including a new separate case that was initiated against Elias "M," effectively shutting down the Secret Service war on the fraud being committed against the telecommunications industry. This got me essentially removed from helping the industry as well as deleting any chance of ever convicting anyone of the fraud scheme associated with the WorldCom and MCI prepaid scam. What a fuckin' joke!

Let me explain the key facts behind the evidence associated with the prepaid calling card case. For starters, it was a conspiracy charge that we indicted them on. With over 20 years of law enforcement experience and a very unique opportunity that most law enforcement professionals rarely have, the suspects were clearly intercepted over government bugs discussing a bust-out scheme, and then admitting to past performance as well as future plans to do the same.

With this key facet in place, the basics need to be identified. So, here is how I understand a conspiracy charge and the "challenges" it brings to a defense team. A conspiracy is basically a broad crime that can sweep up many kinds of conduct, and typically, these types of charges are usually a big challenge to defend in court. A federal criminal defense attorney, who has a client charged with conspiracy, has to be very diligent in investigating the government's evidence and what role the government thinks each person had in the conspiracy. This can be a very daunting task indeed.

In addition, a conspiracy to commit a federal crime happens whenever there is an agreement to commit a specific federal crime between two or more people, and at least one of those people makes some "overt" act to further the conspiracy. Also, the government does not have to prove that there was a written agreement between the coconspirators; instead, basically the prosecutor can prove a conspiracy just by proving that the people it says were involved in the conspiracy were working together to commit some crime.

The general federal conspiracy statute is 18 U.S.C. 371. This statute criminalizes both conspiracies to defraud the United States as well as conspiracies to violate any other provision of federal law. Therefore, one can understand by the text of that provision and clearly see how the two elements work. The statute says that it is a crime if two or more persons conspire either to commit any offense against the United States, or to defraud the United States, or any agency thereof in any manner or for any purpose, and one or more of such persons do any act to effect the object of the conspiracy.

Let me also explain, the courts have held that an individual can be in a conspiracy with another person, even if the two people never meet or interact, as long as they knew the other person was doing something to further the conspiracy. Denny McLain repeatedly stated during his meetings with me that he never met Gotti, and, of course, I didn't comment, since I knew what the conspiracy statute stated on use of such a defense. Now, of course, not ever meeting your coconspirators is most common in a larger, sprawling conspiracy where a central person, or a group of people, and/or an enterprise such as the "syndicate," would coordinate the work of others.

Also fair game, a conspiracy charge has the potential to be abused by the government, and taken to absurd consequences in theory, a conspiracy offense could be committed and prosecuted in federal court merely by having two people agree that they would rob a bank together, and then buy a ski mask to wear in the bank robbery. But let me be crystal clear, the phone card conspiracy charge was nothing remotely close to being abused by the government; in this case, by myself and my team.

One vicious consequence of a conspiracy charge is that a very minor participant in a conspiracy can be swept up in the same case as someone who is much more responsible and culpable for criminal conduct. This is a particularly bad problem in drug conspiracy cases. For example, a person who had a very minor role in a drug conspiracy that involved a significant quantity of drugs can be subject to a mandatory minimum for all the drugs in the conspiracy.

In our case, we have John Gotti Junior discussing the scheme with Anthony Plomitallo on a bug that was planted in a vehicle driven at the time by Plomitallo. We have numerous discussions about the distribution capabilities and the recruitment of those who were considered not only good distributors but also played well with others in the "criminal sandbox." The key players in the prepaid phone card scam, whether as part of an earlier scheme or the one we intercepted, were folks like Denny McLain, Joe "The German" Watts, and Salvatore Scala, to name just a few.

These were bad people who had been doing bad things for a very long time. So the beauty of the wiretaps and bugs planted by OCTF was that John Gotti Junior felt comfortable and compelled to discuss the actual scheme to his driver at a time to be very critical to moving the scheme forward. Travel Cards had just defrauded WorldCom of $90-plus million and they had to file bankruptcy since they were shut off. Since the scheme went so well, they decided to continue it and included other players in the mix. One key player was Denny McLain and his company, Tel Central.

As explained in my earlier chapters, the conversations intercepted made comparisons to the early scheme with the Travel phone cards. As Gotti explained, he wasn't going to do that but rather, whenever a card had issues of potentially being shut down due to nonpayment, they would substitute it with a new card. He saw that with the Travel Card, once the service was cut off, the scheme had no life left, and it had no choice but to terminate.

This $90 million one-time fraud scheme had the Gambino crime family all excited. In the May 28, 1996, conversation, during the peak of the Travel Card era, Gotti explained that as one card faltered another one would take over and that the Liberty Tel card, his card, was going to be one of those cards that we wanted to preserve. These were interesting times, and one mistake could be detrimental. In fact, even the late John Gotti Senior commented in prison about the phone card business. He basically said his son Peter had come to him and said, "Dad, I'm in the phone card business," and with a laugh, Senior said, "What a scam."

We had additional intercepts that mentioned the association of the syndicate with Denny McLain and how he was preparing to "ramp up" service for them. In a written confession and as a cooperating witness, we had Denny's "unnamed" family member provide an outline of the scheme. Now, did we have individuals trying to scam each other? Yes. Did we have the Liberty Tel card minimally involved in the scam? Yes. But with that, we had them dead to right for they were cooked and cooked well.

The investigative work was done mostly by me and a few other agents who had seconds on the job. No one in the New York Field Office had any experience that involved a long-term fraud investigation that targeted the head of an organized crime syndicate. Special Agent Chris F was my only partner, and as I stated earlier, he, like me, had no reason to go home and watch movies. We loved the hunt investigations offered, and prior to Chris joining, I was working this unknown fraud alone. What was especially frustrating to me was the lack of guidance provided to me but the Secret Service to their defense was just too busy with the protection business. Although it is easy to say it is really hard to adopt to such a practice especially when I had come from such a long term investigative culture.

So for instance, in the Secret Service there was a good understanding on how a search warrant should be conducted, but how to get there within the fraud arena, a very limited amount of experience existed among the senior agents. The Service in New York was good with conducting counterfeit cases. This was because the mentality used was strictly buy-and-bust operations. They would dedicate themselves for 2–3 weeks of tireless investigative efforts toward an operation, and hopefully, a protection assignment would not derail the momentum. If one did, it would more likely than not put the case on the back-burner, so to speak. Unless the suspect or note reappeared, it was closed out.

Proactive investigative work was a foreign concept during this time unless it involved a protective intelligence case. The Service expended great effort, time, and resources to conduct thorough investigations toward those who made threats against the president or any person under the Service's protection. The stakes were too high for it to be otherwise.

Forget about the thought of starting a case from the ground up on a known target because the level of fraud was being perpetrated; forget it. These agents were doing, in my opinion, casework simply to stay busy until they were assigned their next protection assignment and nothing more. This was how the agency at the time was structured, and the New York Field Office was no different. The only difference was the size and location of the office. If the office was located in a major city or near the home of a former president, then the mission would have a heavy day-to-day commitment to the protection mission, but this was not the case with our investigative mission. I couldn't get one person to be fully committed to asset forfeiture and/ or understand it. Yet, the NYFO had an asset forfeiture squad. I often felt alone going up against a formidable opponent with very little to no support.

11

Like Oil and Vinegar, Investigations & Protection Don't Mix Well

As time passed, I slowly adapted to some of the clothing and equipment that was a "staple" trademark of the agency and its agents. As an example, we all bought this particular luggage system that every single Secret Service agent owned. I cannot imagine how I would handle this type of luggage system today. The tactical features of this luggage were exceptional, and the luggage itself was extremely durable. Of course, it was all-black and specifically designed for government agents who were on the road more often than not. Long-term sturdiness was the key essential behind the design. Yet, to carry it, you either slung it over your shoulder or you needed to do so by hand.

The people who designed this luggage must have been either body-builders or swimmers who were strong enough to lift this awkwardly designed equipment or probably only needed one bag to carry their swimwear. For us agents who were on the road at times for up to 2–3 weeks, it was horrible. For starters, there were no wheels, and unlike flight attendant luggage where you could attach additional luggage to one main one with wheels, we had no consolidation options. Instead, this ballistic nylon bag with pockets everywhere was designed for all sorts of weapons, ammo, pistols, rifle magazines, flashlights, and handcuffs. However, for the frequent traveler who needed to carry it from point "A" to point "B" through a crowded airport, while wearing a suit, it was impractical at best, and a hindrance at its worst. Yet, for some reason, we all purchased and carried the same luggage. Go figure.

Weeks prior to any presidential trip, the Secret Service begins preparation for all aspects of security surrounding the visit. Therefore, the time that needs to be allocated for the preparation of a visit is the first challenge for agents working a case load. Although their security role is temporary, there is no time to do both assignments well and thus the protection always trumps the investigative work. The agents from the Presidential Protective Division, those who surround the inner circle around the president, work in partnership with the agents from various field offices to provide the necessary protection whenever on the road. What begins is called the "security advance," whereby liaison is conducted with all stakeholders, including the host committee, business owners, local law enforcement, and public safety officials to ensure a cohesive and coordinated effort once the president steps foot off of Air Force One.

It was late August 1996, and as I briefly mentioned in an earlier chapter, as a young agent in the New York Field Office, I, along with fellow agents, were selected to serve as train security. It was not a glamorous position, or a coveted one, for that matter. To be clear, I never came within 30 yards of President Clinton. Nevertheless, it was an absolutely necessary function, albeit a tedious one. It was an election year, and the president was on the way to winning his second term, while I, as a new agent, would serve in the wings, in staircases, back alleys, and along his whistle-stop tour, providing physical middle perimeter security.

We awoke before sunrise every day, boarded a bus, which would transport a group of agents to a train where we would board and take our predetermined positions, usually two per train car. Then we would wait for hours until the president boarded the train and the campaign whistle-stop would begin. The ride was uncomfortable as we were not allowed to sit. When the train would come to a stop or when crowds would gather along the tracks to catch a glimpse of President Clinton, wave, scream, and occasionally carry signs expressing various forms of either love or disdain for the president, we were to stand along each side of an open train car and do our best to scan the environment for threats. This was a difficult task as we were on a moving train!

When the train would finally come to a stop, the crowds gathered were often in the thousands. Again, we were not allowed to leave those damn train cars . . . So we did what we were tasked to do; namely, scan the crowds for unusual activity, out-of-normal behavior, and if noticed, call it out over a radio. I recall the feeling of boredom while sitting in those hot train cars, feeling hungry, yet all would cease and be replaced by a flow of adrenaline when we would stop in every small town and witness the vibrancy of the people gathered to witness a glimpse of history.

The public euphoria was at times contagious as bands would play loud, upbeat music, the people happy to be a part of something greater than themselves and bigger than the small towns from whence they came. What they witnessed though was the finished product of weeks filled with intense negations, long hours of security advance work, weeks away from home, and, of course, the mundane routine and boredom. Boredom and routine were quite often the hallmark and vulnerability of an agent's work on protection; yet, we all found it within ourselves to fight the dangers of complacency to once again turn it on once the train stopped and the doors opened . . .

I was experiencing my first real investigative withdrawal and confusion with the experience. One day I am working the streets wearing jeans, a T-shirt, and a baseball cap; another day, I am wearing a suit and an earpiece that is connected to a handheld radio. How can this be? I remember asking myself these very questions. If you're working a case, deeply involved in an investigation, how do you just walk away and do something totally different and basically have no contact with suspects, witnesses, or government attorneys, and be considered a real investigator?

I saw the value and higher purpose in the protection mission, but felt that the continuous interchange between protective and investigative assignments prevented one from fully immersing themselves in the intricacies of a complex investigation. Yet, regardless of the protection demands, I continued to make cases, usually during my "off-duty" hours. The cases I worked on produced "linear" results. Basic techniques were used, and I would compare it to a smash-and-grab mentality at best. Rarely did one have the opportunity to really identify the "organization" behind the targeted group, and in all cases, the approach taken was very similar to a police squad level with the only difference, we were enforcing federal law.

I recall that immediately after the Gotti investigation, my protection orders came to help safeguard the fifth president of the People's

Republic of China, Jiang Zemin's visit to New York City to meet with the POTUS. Manpower was needed; a call was made to everyone on deck, including me. I was now made available to any and all requests for protection work as I no longer had my investigation to cultivate. I recall seeing the agent who coordinated the protection operations squad, a tall and a physically imposing figure, looking down at me with a sinister-like smile as the news that I was no longer "hands off" came to his attention. Now, talk about a "mameluke."

I loved the guy, but if he couldn't see that I was working my ass off during "hands off," then what can I say? Anyway, on that particular assignment, I spent 4 days on a 12-hour shift standing in the fire stairwell of the Waldorf Astoria hotel. During those very long hours in a hot stairwell, with nothing to do but think, I quickly realized that my passion of working sophisticated cases had come to an end. During these painfully mundane and long days, I was accompanied by various police officers of the New York City Police Department's (NYPD) Emergency Services Unit, an elite tactical team. I never had the same officer twice; makes sense . . . The NYPD had 38,000 or so officers at the ready.

Each time I would speak to the new officer assigned to my post, I was thrilled by the fact that we would maybe have an hour tops' worth of new discussions before that new experience became a dud. The extremely painful part came after the initial hour, when there was nothing more to ask each other. At that point, both the officer and I would retreat to opposite corners where there was partial light so that if we decided to rest a bit by closing our eyes, of course, all while still standing, no one would catch us in the act. The hours spent in that stairwell were very painful, and for someone like me whose mind always raced, this was a slow death sentence, and I was unwilling to accept it. At times, I would count various things to keep me busy, such as cracks on the stairs—anything to pass the time.

The hours seemed to never pass when on such assignments, and it had been some time since I have actually stood for so long. Your mind would race. My God, you would try to think of so many things just to keep yourself occupied. This was a time that pagers were used so some folks would send themselves messages or use various noises or clicks on the secure radio that was attached to your ear and sleeve. All little tricks to keep oneself occupied. Then there were the problems at home that would grind at you. I never had that issue but did see agents go on post, and as they would be heading to their assignment, you could overhear them discussing the problem at home on a phone or a borrowed cell, and it would always end with "Hey, I got to go. Call you tomorrow." No one really had any freedom when they were on post. They would assign a relief agent, but to be honest, I never got relieved.

After the Gotti case, I was promoted by ATSAIC Weaver to be one of his team leaders in the squad. I was very proud of the acknowledgment and excited to help new agents who wanted to work criminal cases. We had a mix of agents from the private sector, state, and local law enforcement agencies with a broad range of experiences. One thing about the New York Field Office . . . No one really stayed around for long since the protection machine always required fresh blood, and folks were constantly being assigned to a respective detail. The typical career track basically had you going from the field office to a protection detail, then for a touch-and-go at headquarters, and then back out to a field office, or possibly back to protection.

As I mentioned earlier, Chris was my partner at ECTF. We both had apartments in Riverdale, New York. He had served in the military and was active during the Persian Gulf War. As a United States Army Airborne Paratrooper assigned to the 82nd Airborne, he had seen a great deal as a young paratrooper. Chris was the nephew to the director of the Secret Service, Lew Merletti, a fact he never discussed or tried to exploit. He stood at about 6 feet, had blondish-brown hair, was clean-shaven, in great shape, and always willing and ready to work. Chris was the quiet type, but I made him laugh constantly. We enjoyed many great times together, both on and off the job.

I was getting a bit frustrated because the "hands-off" status that I was in due to the Gotti case was over. That status allowed me to work cases and not be available for temporary protection assignments. Every time something would come across my desk, I had just enough time to either assign it or deal with it for a day or two. Weaver knew that I was getting frustrated and reminded me that my time was coming to an end in the office and unless I opted out, which meant stay in New York and embark on the typical Secret Service career path, I would be given assignments to get me ready and exposed to either the Presidential Protective Division (PPD) or the Vice Presidential Protective Division (VPPD).

I was not interested in protection. So I looked for ways to distance myself from the work. At the time, there was a program directed toward larger field offices where an agent could "opt out," which allowed you to stay in New York your entire career. Although I was no longer in the running for a promotion, this got me out of doing full-time protection, as well as it basically sent a negative message of me back to Washington, and my temporary protection assignments did not end. I was still part of a rotation like all the other 200-plus agents in New York, and so this option, although somewhat attractive, did not satisfy my needs, which were to solve sophisticated long-term financial crime cases that involved the Mafia.

So I continued to plug along, days turning into weeks that turned into months, and I would go from working various financial crime cases to random protective assignments. The year 1998 ended with a mix of foreign dignitary protection assignments, working post-standing assignments for President Clinton and Vice President Gore, and on a personal note, my getting a divorce. It was early 1999 when I received a call from one of the private sector contacts within the utility industry. He informed me that they were having an issue in Harlem with some unusual activity at a particular apartment.

The activity was gouging the utility service illegally. So I spoke to Weaver and with his permission, assigned the case to my partner Chris and another fairly new agent who was very talented in cybersecurity, Peter Cavicchia. The case involved a West African ring that used stolen credit cards to purchase both long-distance phone time as well as merchandise. I enjoyed the new role as a team leader providing guidance and direction, but my enjoyment truly came from seeing this new wave of younger agents think through the investigative process and making sound decisions. We immediately presented the case to ASUSA Eric Bruce and Michael Kim, two outstanding attorneys, who, today, work together at a very successful law firm in Manhattan.

Anyway, in my investigative world, as a case agent, I would track the finances and work up the food chain to see who was running and directing the operation. By going down this road and influencing the agents to do the same, I knew that it would be a terrible mistake and that the Service would totally make a mess of the case by innocently trumping the case with protective assignments. In no time, they would ship us to various protection assignments and a week or two later, try to resume and resurrect a case.

I kept my opinions to myself and coached the agents by keeping the case small, focusing on the immediate targets, and closing the case at that point. This went completely against my investigative grain, but

I had no choice but to do so since the agency was not geared for a marathon investigation, one where the investigative strategy as well as identifying the assets from the criminal proceeds was the focus and methodology. I personally knew that any attempt to do so would be met with failure, and seeing how we were completely not prepared for the work requirement the Gotti case presented, I was not willing to make that mistake again . . .

We were trying to obtain evidence to execute a search warrant at this apartment in Harlem where most of the residents within a two-block radius were from West Africans. The target was, at the time, unknown but in the end, we were able to identify the main suspect through standard checks as "Seck." Seck Seynabou was a woman from Africa and the listed tenant of the apartment. She was later identified as one of fraudsters. On our initial surveillance of the location, we noticed from the exterior part of the building an unusual phone line connected to others and running through the window to her apartment.

I believe we had a representative of the phone company who was also a task force member along with us, and he helped identify that someone was tapping into the phone lines of other legitimate customers. With our partnerships in the private sector, it was clear this line was not authorized, and now we needed to gain entry, just enough to get a glimpse of the situation inside and obviously obtain enough probable cause to secure a search warrant . . .

So Chris and I posed as Con Ed workers; we had the equipment and the IDs back in the squad in storage, so why not. We had a simple plan, usually the best way . . . We go to each apartment and count the rooms and square footage so we can supply free air conditioners . .

. It was the middle of a blistering hot summer and free window units for those that qualify sounded like a good plan.

So as we made our way to the building, wouldn't you know it—a fuckin' Con Ed truck is parked 100 feet from the entrance area of the building, and we were caught by surprise, and before we could turn around and get out of Dodge, one of the supervisors spots us and I immediately walked up to him and shoved him back in the truck all the while showing him my badge so he knew this was not something we needed him to screw up. We got past that obstacle, and then we headed up to the building. The truck outside made the whole thing authentic, except for the outdated uniforms and hard hats, which is what the Con Ed worker spotted.

We started by going to all the floors below the target one and finished at the top floor offering the rebate. We did not want Seck to think she was targeted, and we needed to look as real and authentic as possible. We went as far as purchasing a few AC units in the event we needed to return to the apartment for the purpose of obtaining more evidence. Well, once we got to the target apartment, Seck opened the door. She had a heavy accent, but before long, I was able to bullshit her enough to get past the door/entry level.

As we moved forward inside the apartment discussing the rebate, using measuring tape around windows and began our acting audition, we immediately spotted a notebook pad and in plain view, handwritten on the page were at least a dozen credit card numbers, with various names and Social Security numbers. We could easily see numerous phone cards on the table. Connected to the mysterious line coming through the window was both a phone and fax machine. This was enough evidence for a search warrant; the place was a mess. We thanked Seck, who was demanding her AC unit, and we promised after checking our calendar that some time either Monday or Tuesday of next week we would have her unit delivered.

Within 48 hours, the search warrant was granted, the operations plan completed and approved. Some agents had just completed their protection assignments and now were changing into jeans and throwing on their unique dark blue bulletproof vests with the golden Secret Service Star on the front. They dressed as I briefed them on the plan.

The local police precinct was notified, but since this was a task force, we had every local and federal presence within the squad, so notification was not difficult to execute. I had my entry team, and I had my arrest and evidence team, and I had my outside perimeter team. We were set, and when we hit, we hit hard and fast so that no one inside the apartment had a chance to think . . . Hey, these were Secret Service men and women in the best shape, with the very best equipment, and above all, the industry was there to provide us any and all details so that no evidence went without proper review. We did well. There were a total of six individuals in the apartment, including Seck, and combined with arrests and evidence collected, we had thousands of individual credit card accounts compromised and hundreds of thousands of dollars of merchandise seized.

This was a well-organized ring of thieves and fraudsters using all sorts of folks to collect information on valid credit card holders. Some of them were customers that frequented the African stores for merchandise. Others victims were tourists that would take the bus tours in the city and not know that within minutes of either entering or exiting the bus, or maybe sitting or standing on the bus, their wallets were stolen and their credit cards compromised by this sophisticated group.

My chapter in New York was now over with the Gotti case behind me, and a bit frustrated with the Secret Service, I called back to the resident agent in charge in Milan, Italy. His name was Al Concordia, and one day months earlier, I was looking for hotels to stay in the area and was introduced to him by his office assistant Marisa. Marisa a wonderful woman who has passed, and she was absolutely the life of the office. Anyway, Al and I immediately connected, and I asked him if the invitation to being assigned in Milan would still be open. He assured me it was and after letting Weaver know of my intentions, he spoke to the SAIC in New York, Chip Smith, and the rest was history. Although Milan was not my final destination, Rome had a SAIC, and he trumped the RAC. I eventually received orders to report to Rome.

It was just weeks prior to my transfer to Rome, February 29, 2000. I was packed and staying at the hotel nearby the World Trade Center. After hours, I would meet with my female acquaintances since I knew it would be years until I would see them again. I was ready to testify in front of a blind judge, the Honorable Richard Conway Casey, who had his trusty Labrador that would sporadically growl at the defendant whenever she spoke in French. The hearing was to determine whether the defendant would be released and allowed to surrender her passport to the court.

The defendant's attorney began by apologizing to the judge asking for the opportunity to explain his position. He was preparing to request the courts not remand Seck but rather release her and allow her time to return and surrender her passport, which, by the defendant's statement, was nowhere to be found. To make matters worse, Roland unsuccessfully attempted to taint our reputation with an unfortunate incident that had happened weeks earlier when two Secret Service agents from the New York Field Office were caught lying about a witness. The incident made the news, and it was embarrassing. Roland wanted to know if I was one of those agents.

The Honorable Judge Casey had a reputation for being pro-law enforcement and did not like the public defender's tactics. So when Roland opened his argument by asking for permission to speak, the judge immediately interrupted him and stated, "It better be good, Mr. Thau." So the moment Roland responded by saying "Am I to conclude from that short remark that the court has already..." Casey didn't allow him to finish his sentence and got a quick response from Casey who fired back, "You can conclude anything you want, but you're suggesting that I drop it as a condition." The exchange that followed was intense, to say the least, and I must say, I was laughing on the inside, but no one knew it.

I was in Rome maybe 6 months and needed to return to New York City for the Seck trial. I was thrilled to return home since I missed my friends and the girlfriends. Rome was not easy for so many reasons that I will explain in my later chapters, and so getting back on the government's dime was a big treat. We prepped for the case, and once trial began, there was a serious tone that overtook all of us. Court started in much the same manner as our last engagement with Seck and Thau. The court-appointed attorney, who was a disheveled older man who looked a lot like Bernie Sanders, was bent on getting that aha! moment. It was my turn on the stand, and as soon as I did, Roland began to pepper me with questions, hopelessly looking for some clue or break that would turn the trial in favor of his client.

Honestly, it was useless, almost like looking for a needle in a haystack. The case was airtight, and everything we did was absolutely aboveboard. So when Roland asked his questions, I was extremely well prepared, confident, and although never cocky, I was enjoying the sparing that was taking place in the courtroom. Each time he asked a question, stumbling over his words at times, I would turn toward the jury and provide an answer while looking into the eyes of each and every juror. I would fully answer his questions, providing detailed descriptions of the evidence or circumstances that led to a particular conclusion. Roland was obviously frustrated and had no choice but to concede to the loss.

I was now officially done with my investigative work in New York; my part on this case was also completed. It was time to head back to Rome, and within days of my arrival, the Assistant United States Attorney called me to thank me for my efforts. This call was followed up with an official letter of appreciation sent to the New York office and Rome Field Office. They were so pleased with the outcome; Seck was convicted on all counts. It was clearly obvious to them that the jury was not only impressed with the investigative facts, but also with me. I didn't realize it then, but reflecting back, they were all so attentive to whenever I spoke. AUSA Michael Kim explained that the jury during deliberations had asked to see me one more time and he had to inform them that I was on my way to Rome. Worried, he had asked if there was any concerns; however, they were basically starstruck and said, "No, we just wanted to see him one last time."

12

"While in Rome do as the Romans . . ."

If you have not visited Rome, Italy, you need to book a trip to that wonderful city and spend a week living and eating like a real Romano! During my transfer there, I absolutely indulged in the culture. I had the advantage of my Italian upbringing in New York. I can tell you within months I had shed all my bulky American suits and shoes and was wearing things like a scarf around my neck as if I were a native, wrapping it in a European loop. My friends would make fun of me upon my return to the States for this particular newfound style. I purchased a motorcycle, one of the most luxurious racing bikes built for touring; an all-gray 2000 BMW 1200RS. At the time, I was basically the only one in Rome who had one, and everyone would stare at it when I rode it to work wearing a matching colored helmet, always dressed to impress.

The social gatherings in Rome were amazing, and during the summer months, embassy diplomats had access to the ambassador's pool at Villa Taverna. For me, it was basically within walking distance from my apartment in Parioli, a very affluent neighborhood that housed many of the homes of the foreign ambassadors. I was provided an apartment suited for a family of four, and being a single man, this was more than enough room. The American Embassy in Rome is located on Via Veneto, and our "annex" was just a few blocks away, so although the place was secure, it was a bit less pronounced to the tourists who flocked Via Veneto year-round.

I was assigned a government car outfitted with diplomatic plates used for official duty, but on my personal time, I drove my "other" jewel, a red 1984 five-speed Porsche 911 Carrera. It still had New York license plates, and on the weekends, I would switch from the motorcycle to the car, depending on the weather conditions. The car was also an absolute looker, and it had a badass whale tail to further impress. It was completely refurbished with attention to the slightest detail. There wasn't a month that would go by where I wouldn't tuck or pull something on her just to keep her in "mint" condition. The car had a Targa top that was always off whenever I drove through the beautiful region of Italy known as La Toscana.

With custom stainless steel Haywood & Scott Crossover exhausts letting everyone know that we were coming, it was an absolute blast to drive. I particularly enjoyed making the doorman to my apartment building smile as I would come out of the garage and up the driveway. He would hear me coming and as I "crept" up to look to my left making sure there were no cars coming, he would be smiling with anticipation while holding a broom. He held that broom and smile until I completely disappeared from view as I entered Piazza Euclide. As I made my way down the road, the parked cars alongside the narrow road would sound off their alarms. They would all go off, set off from the vibration and loud rumbling coming from my pipes.

What was absolutely intoxicating was the experience I had with the

Italian cuisine. Yes, I was Italian, and we cooked authentic, but there was something different coming out of the kitchens and restaurants in Rome. It was all absolutely amazing in Rome, and I enjoyed every meal and every minute. I quickly became good friends with my Italian counterparts who were also in the same line of business: law enforcement. Stefano, Salvatore, and Marco, all unique; they had great knowledge of the food and culture and wanted me to also experience it. These guys were proud to be Italian, knew exactly where to eat, and knew how to not spend a boatload of money doing so. Going to dinner with these fine men was always a spectacular time.

We would always start our evening with an *aperativo* used to entice the stomach's appetite. Gaining an appetite was never an issue for me. Then the next item would be a little *assaggino*, which, loosely translated, means a small taste of something delicious! We would usually have some perfectly cured prosciutto, which is Italian "air-dried" ham that is served thinly sliced. It is typically served on a wooden board that housed other "mouthwatering" items like homemade bread drizzled with extra virgin olive oil, local cheeses, and an assortment of other delights.

What made these evenings fantastic was that in Italy, having dinner was an absolute performance. The locals did not look for a quick bite but rather quality, and they understood what quality meant in food. Whenever in a restaurant you were never rushed since the protocol was not to turn the table but to give the client an experience. Italians are also very picky of what they eat, and above all, want to enjoy their company at the table. Therefore the typical dinner was a minimum 2-plus hour event. But besides these long dinners, I really enjoyed watching people.

Whenever I had a weekend to myself and there wasn't a "friend" visiting me, I would spend the weekends at Piazza Navone, sitting at an outdoor café and pretend I was reading a newspaper, all the while checking out the locals, the tourists, and those in between. I mean, it was absolutely wonderful to sit there at various times either having a cappuccino with little pastries resembling croissants called *corneti*, or during the latter part of the day grabbing a Panini filled with mortadella from the local street vendor. The experience was fantastic, only to be surpassed by the euphoria felt by working a really good case supporting a foreign government law enforcement team identifying bad guys who were trying to get over on U.S. citizens . . .

Obviously, I was ready for a change. The NYFO had nothing more to offer, and after working such an intense case, I just wanted to make a corrective action in my life. Although drained emotionally, I was physically in my best shape ever. I had to recalibrate myself and needed an assignment that would bring the excitement back into my life, and I thought the Rome office would be the right place for me. In New York, while waiting for my orders, I jogged every morning. The running path alongside the West Side Highway was what I loved, and it was a routine for me. I avoided our gym, which was on the ninth floor at 7 World Trade Center. There, the Service had cutting-edge weight lifting equipment necessary to keep the men and women who protect the president in top shape. Nonetheless, I preferred being outside running along the Hudson River. The run was always followed up with a set of 100 push-ups and sit-ups until I couldn't do them anymore.

It's Monday morning in Rome, Italy; I start that particular morning by quietly grabbing my shorts and a T-shirt. In my bed, still sleeping, was my blond, German-born, Lufthansa flight attendant who I had met on a trip to the Middle East. Typically, I would arrange for the woman who would spend a weekend in Rome with me to leave on a Sunday night so that I could prepare for the week's mission. This time, I had slipped, and although I was being a bit selfish, decided to keep my "lady friend" in Rome for an extra night. Anyway, I quickly hide my weapon and credentials and made myself a quick café macchiato prior to my 30-minute jog, followed up with a half-dozen sprints up a flight of stairs. I always enjoyed the drill and the initial pour of sweat that followed.

After a last-minute romp in the bedroom, my friend departed by cab, and I grabbed my government car and headed off to work. Before entering the official car, a late-model BMW, I inspected it and examined my "field-improvised" security measures. These were installed as countermeasures every Friday night, knowing it was going to be there parked for the weekend. These measures were taken in hopes to help me determine if the car was compromised in any way. This is a country where car bombs are the preferred choice. After a quick review and being convinced that all was good, I headed toward Fiumicino airport to board the Alitalia flight bound for Bucharest, Romania.

Romania was a very depressed country with a great deal of poverty. Immediately upon landing, you see the poverty and lack of resources. As the Alitalia flight I was on approached the runway, on both sides of the airstrip I saw abandoned airplanes, commercial and military ones that all looked similar to a roadside carcass left to rot. As the predators would systematically eat away at the remains of a dead animal, the planes had similar characters. They had engine parts missing, some had parts of the fuselage missing. I could not believe that they allowed this to be the first visual image experienced by the foreign visitor. However, this was Romania, and they were under communist rule. I guess they had bigger issues, as I was soon going to find out.

As I departed the airport, I began my countersurveillance measures, hoping to minimize the impact, or at the very least, make it difficult to be followed. As soon as I left the airport, I would be completely surrounded by children of all ages begging for money. They were all in one way or another deformed and all so cute. My heart would break every time I encountered them. Today, I sometimes see those faces whenever I look into the eyes of my own kids. It pained me to see these suffering children, and in the not-too-far distance, I could see their handlers. It took extreme strength not to give them money in the vain hope I would possibly prevent the cycle of abuse to continue.

Not everyone followed this reasoning, as other foreigners handed out money. If you weren't careful, the mothers would also approach with the goal of pick pocketing you. The buildings were completely run-down, and although the countryside was beautiful, the means in which folks were cared for was equal to that of animals. Hospitals, dental facilities, and overall public facilities were poorly equipped, and sanitary conditions were at best, marginal.

During my travels to Bucharest, I stayed at the Hilton Hotel, and whenever I got there, I would initiate a series of drills on my part to confuse the Romanian intelligence. I would be issued a set of keys and would return to the front desk claiming the room was dirty and force them to switch me out of the current room. Then I would always leave the TV on, and, of course, use the do not disturb sign. At times, to ensure there was no one in my room, or heading there, I would use the stairs, and then hop on the elevator and return back to the room. In the many attempts, there was that one occasion after switching rooms that I found a technician in the room. I had obviously surprised him and his team, and although he was "working" on my TV, it was clear he was there for something else.

The one thing I was extremely fortunate to have on my side in Romania were the two Romanian law enforcement counterparts I met and worked exclusively with throughout my time there. It was because of them that I was extremely successful and able to fulfill Special Agent in Charge Ralph Gonzalez's demand: "Son, I want us to have presence in Romania." I never felt concerned about my personal safety. I often think about our times together. Tibus and Cristian, these two guys, were serious investigators and dear friends who protected me from corrupt officers. Unlike Bulgaria, in Romania, I knew who the enemy was and believed success was being made in the field. Both men were based out of the Romanian police headquarters element and were both specialized in computer crimes.

I met Tibus in his office, and I must say, the image of what it looked like took me by surprise. Here I am a U.S. Special Agent with all the latest technology and equipment, and as we can all attest to, we are always complaining about our resources, or the lack thereof. Well, let me tell you the Romanian police, Tibus, at the time, built his computer from various scrap parts. If you weren't warned ahead of time that it was an official government computer, you would think it was a pile of junk ready to be thrown out. As soon as possible and with headquarters' approval, we made sure that we shipped Tibus some computer equipment.

The man was sincere, honest, and he truly wanted to do good, and how fortunate for me to meet such an investigator. Soon after meeting Tibus, I was introduced to Cristian who was from another section of the police department. Cristian was a friend of Tibus, who was also a fantastic computer wizard who wanted to make cases. Cristian was very quiet and like many people in that region, afraid that one day their relationship with the U.S. would be disrupted by either corruption or by communist hardliners. You can see the concern in their eyes, but with all that said, these men were courageous and ready to fight.

Soon after forging our friendship, we had our opportunity. I was in Rome sitting at my desk one day and the phone rings, an agent from Secret Service Headquarters calls and talks about a cyber case that is originating out of Romania. The referral call went right to me since I was tasked to get Romania staffed with a full-time Secret Service presence. The agent on the other end of the phone explained that the home page to the Thrift Savings Plan was recently defaced, and the attack originated in Romania. I requested that all the details be sent to me, and within hours from the call, I made contact with the Romanian company that hosted the IP address used to deface the site.

After initiating other investigative steps as well as contacting our folks at Interpol, I eventually speak with the owner of the server in Romania. In broken English, he provides me with helpful information. I contacted Tibus and explained to him the issue, and he was immediately receptive. I provided copies of the data we had collected, and in a matter of hours, Tibus was certain that the incident had taken place in Timisoara, Romania, and that he was ready to travel there to interview suspects. I thanked him, briefed my boss and the folks in Washington, and packed a quick bag as the next morning I was on the first flight to Bucharest, Romania.

After arriving in Bucharest and getting briefed by Tibus, the next morning, I take a flight to the city of Timisoara where I hone in on finding the actual hackers. Tibus, due to political reasons, was unable to accompany me. Although only a little over an hour, it was a "shocker" of a flight. Passengers were allowed to smoke onboard. This was bad enough—until I noticed farm animals were allowed passage. A large goat was onboard. Operated by Tarom, the old plane had curtains on the windows, the type you would find in an old country kitchen. We boarded from the rear, and I noticed that the tires on the plane had visible white treads exposed. I was completely prepared for the worse incident possible with this flight and could not wait to get off. We were basically flying on an old Tarom turboprop plane with a capacity of no more than 50 people. The whole experience made me very nervous.

Timisoara is one of the largest cities in Romania with a little more than 300,000 inhabitants. The city was always in the center of economic development and one of the first cities in Europe to have electric streetlights. Now, in terms of living standards, it ranks fourth in the country with foreign investment always knocking on "her" door; Timisoara has had significant foreign investment. It all didn't matter in comparison to the rest of the world; it was third world at best.

Within hours of my arrival in Timisoara, I was informed that my Bucharest police team of Tibus and Cristian would meet me the following day. I needed them as they were my only lifelines when it comes to understanding the crime and finding something that will tie the crime to a punishment. Without them, we would be totally lost and run the risk of looking like a bunch of fools. I was doubtful in the competency and commitment of the police department officials to adequately investigate and support me. I found people I trusted and wanted them involved. I did not want to go through the normal dog-and-pony show, having to babysit government officials, wine and dine them, and at the end, it is all for naught—simply a waste of my time. I wanted to get to work.

Everywhere you go in Romania, including Timisoara, you would see folks begging with some horrible physical deformities. The people are known as Romani ("Roma" gypsies). I was later told not to pay any mind to those begging because it was not only depressing, but it needed to be ignored since it was really all just a big scam. The truth of the matter is their own family members deformed many of their children at birth. These people were called gypsies, looking for ways to make money. So to gain sympathy, they did these terrible things to their own children when they were all very young. A complete tragedy, one that to this day, I still see those deformed children and people haunting me in my dreams.

I felt for the first time powerless. How could this be? Here I am in Romania, this special agent of the Secret Service, everyone excited to see me, and the first wave of injustice hits me . . . and all I can do is stare hopelessly back. It was difficult, but I quickly composed myself and ignored the warnings. Whenever I could, without being discovered, I gave the children money. At times, it was done with the goal of masking the true amount of money donated.

I remember one instance where a child barefoot in the middle of the winter begging with his hands out hoping to collect some money. I grabbed him with one quick swift swoop with one arm as his father, from a distance, watched, a typical tactic used by these evil people. I rushed him into a shoe store, and as I purchased a pair of shoes for him, and pretended to check how they fit, I slipped him one Romanian 100.000 Leu, which is about $20 U.S. The boy, now being out from the cold, with his rosy red cheeks, had a smile from ear to ear. He was happy but not for the shoes I bought him but for the money he understood was all his.

When I arrived at my hotel in Timisoara, a stunning brunette greeted me, and with delight, I have her accompany me to my room. Unlike in the United States, there were no rules to worry about, and with little said, I engaged her sexually, and she was all about it. Within minutes, we were on the bed and with her perfect body pressed against mine I stopped at nothing. After a quick romp, she fixed her clothing and left, and I grabbed a quick shower and met the colonel and several of his men in the lobby. We ordered food and, of course, drinks, and with a translator, got very little accomplished since he had a hard time understanding how anyone could steal anything unless they were physically present. The concept of cybercrime was an alien concept.

Computers, for these guys, represented nothing but a paperweight. I needed to bide my time until my counterparts from Bucharest arrived. What was also developing was a strong response from Secret Service headquarters, and within hours, several agents from headquarters were on a plane to join me. The headquarters' support was merely more of a political presence. By the time they arrived, my Romanian counterparts I was waiting on had identified the suspects, and we all drove to their homes.

The next steps were easy. The two young hackers, who were in their teens, had had done all the hacking from a local cybercafé, which, at the time, was well known around Romania. They confessed and explained that they would use stolen credit card information obtained from the Internet black market and used the computers from the café to launch their attacks. Within several hours of debriefing the boys, they agreed to work for the Romanian police, and we financed their activities. It was fantastic, and not to mention, we now looked like huge heroes. The media picked up on the partnership forged between the U.S. Secret Service and Romanian police, the U.S. Embassy was excited, and I was pleased to be a part of their team!

Now, unlike Rome, and later in Bulgaria, I had absolutely no weapon assigned to me while working in Romania. This made me vulnerable, to say the least. Nonetheless, as I stated earlier, my Romanian counterparts were honest, hardworking law enforcement officers whom I trusted and who protected me. They soon introduced me to Victor, who was a local up-and-coming politician who was a brand-new prosecutor. These men combined were willing and able to help me address the growing cyber concerns we had in the United States. For example, Romania programmers in the early 2000s were among the most sought after in the world.

As large international IT companies slowly turned to the East European country, they focused on taking advantage of the strong computing and language skills coupled with cheap labor that the country provided. Yet, its computer literacy is not without its dark side. The country had, at the time, an unenviable reputation as a hotbed for computer fraud and a large community of hackers. The "legitimate" IT is one of Romania's fastest growing export sectors with turnover of about 1 billion euros. Also, roughly 90 percent, about 1,000 IT companies in Romania today, are foreign-owned, and the government hopes exports will reach 1 billion euros in the next couple of years.

At the time, no one would have realized this phenomenon, and today, Romania, in my opinion, is the biggest single source of online auction fraud in the world, a multimillion-dollar industry that scams people using Web sites like eBay. It is very organized. They create fake accounts all to trick people into thinking they are insured. If law enforcement could focus on the Romanians and stop this activity, the amount of online fraud would drop significantly. Some experts say that approximately 70 percent of software used in Romania is pirated, and that "salesmen" still visit office buildings in central Bucharest to sell pirated CDs and DVDs.

What was amazing was that many of the hackers I investigated hoped through their hacks they would be recognized and offered positions of employment with companies and/or foreign governments. The Romanian hacking community is quite large, and they basically see the computer as their "ticket out" of the country. Even today, it is still considered the easiest way to get a better paying job abroad. The Secret Service today, I am proud to say, has proven quite adept and successful at identifying and targeting these Romanian hackers. Within the year of my presence in Romania, the Secret Service had needed justification in opening an office, and within no time at all, the office in Bucharest was staffed with a supervisor and an agent who spoke Romanian. Our presence was recognized, and it was time now for me to find a new mission!

13

Kill the Informant and If You Can, Kill the Agent as Well

It was a cold day, and I was sitting alone in a café located in the lobby of an old but luxurious hotel in downtown Sofia. I was waiting patiently for an important meeting to begin, slowly sipping on an espresso that had a terrible aftertaste, an all-too-common theme in Bulgaria. I missed the joy of having my café in the beautiful city of Rome, where there was equally as much fun in watching the bartenders making a cappuccino, as each cup represented a work of art, to watching the people mill about.

Now, this particular meeting that I was about to have was different than all the others I had while assigned in Bulgaria. For starters, I had countersurveillance support that was extended to me through Roberto, the assistant regional security officer at the American Embassy. Roberto was a friend who always supported me whenever he could. I was dressed in my usual street attire: a long thinblack trench coat I bought in Istanbul, Turkey, jeans, and my square-toed black biker boats. Tucked under my black Italian-made turtleneck sweater was my .380 sig, and on my left wrist, I wore my signature

Secret Service Rolex. I looked more like a gangster than law enforcement, but there was no doubt to those in the Bulgarian underworld who I was.

I was a bit nervous this time. The meeting was orchestrated by Deputy Minister of Interior Boyko Borrisov, who had become a close partner in my fight to bring some sort of order and instill a semblance of genuine initiative from my counterparts in the Bulgaria National Police. I did my best to work with them and be inclusive, but this time was different. It had to be. I did not include them in my meeting, nor were they involved in any of the searches and negotiations that led up to the meeting. I had grown increasingly frustrated since arriving in Bulgaria 4 months prior. All meetings with my police counterparts were filled with empty promises, and in my opinion, a complete waste of time.

I had some "incentives," namely financial, in my back pocket that if and when the time was right, I could lay them on the negotiating table. I held off initially since I knew that the moment the funds were released, I would never see any real progress or change from the police. Therefore, I played the same "cat-and-mouse" game we had engaged in for the past 4 months. Whenever I would meet "the three stooges," the major, the colonel, and the general, all from the police headquarters command in Sofia, I did exactly what they did. I would always start by praising them. I would laugh and joke with them, and in the end, provide them little to no information on what I was doing, nor did I task them running out any substantive investigative leads.

I knew that any lead I provided was going to be immediately compromised. It was also obvious to me that most, if not all, of the counterfeit plant suppressions the police were conducting were, in my opinion, absolutely staged. Since I never suffered fools lightly, I preferred not to be involved with the "pomp and circumstance," then from out of the blue, I would receive a call to meet at police headquarters, and upon arrival, be scuffled into a room, get briefed on a case, handed a counterfeit note to examine, and ultimately, remain wondering if this was just some staged occurrence.

My solution to being partnered with this corrupt group of Bulgarian law enforcement folks was to basically start selecting my own team from scratch. This proved to be almost impossible to achieve, but I was stuck and needed to do something. I first teamed up with the attorneys from both U.S. Treasury and Department of Justice, who, like me, were assigned to the American Embassy. Their joint focus was on improving Bulgarian criminal statutes, the "rule of law," so to speak. Together, we identified the gaps in the Bulgarian criminal procedure code and honed in on a strategy to fix what we could. We attempted to "decipher" the strict rules behind information sharing, and in order to do so, we met with prominent folks in all sectors of banking, finance, and security to discuss the process and a way forward.

As I began to meet these people from various government and private sector companies, I picked and latched onto those who had similar viewpoints and were equally, if not more, frustrated with the process. These were nationals who appeared generally excited over the American presence and displayed a willingness to help improve the rule of law in their beloved country.

It was very difficult to find leaders within the group that had the ability or autonomy to demonstrate any semblance of independent thought. The main reason for this was the ever-lurking threat of repercussions they faced from their government. This obstacle, and being placed in Bulgaria, in essence, with little to no support from my own agency, made my tasking almost impossible. Hands down, this assignment was a huge challenge, and I was not as successful as I needed to be.

This, however, did not prevent me from trying to make a difference. I attended speaking engagements to address the areas in need for improvement; I worked with American Embassy assets, and eventually, was able to cultivate a few confidential informants. Looking back, it was unfortunate but during my time in Bulgaria, I was unable to find an honest investigator, and ultimately, this really limited my progress.

My appointment was late so I continued to sip on my bad-tasting coffee. He was known on the streets as the "Dimata Rusnaka" aka "The Russian," but his actual name was Dimitri Minev, one of the founders of SIC insurance company. SIC, the organization, was actually engaged in extortion, racketeering, trafficking of humans and drugs, money laundering, and other illegal activities. My meeting with Minev was about one of his earners, Petar "Peter" Simenov. Dimitri Minev was absolutely no joke. He was a very serious gangster who was associated with the Russian Mafia. He was indeed a ruthless man whose reputation for such had no equal in the criminal world of Bulgaria.

I immediately spot Dimitri as he exited his vehicle, an armored Mercedes SUV, trailed by another vehicle of similar make and antiballistic capacity. Several hulking bodyguards who were known to carry compact semiautomatic machine guns accompanied him. My sig was absolutely no match. He approached the table, and I stood to shake his hand, and in almost perfect English, he said hello and apologized for being late. Although forewarned, I was amazed at his command of the English language. We started with a bit of small talk. He asked me if I was able to enjoy my stay in Sofia, and how much longer I planned to stay. I used the lead by informing him that my stay depended upon when Peter Simenov was planning to cooperate and return to the United States to face justice.

Dimitri didn't respond but rather told me how he owns property in America and how he was having issues obtaining his visa. At that moment, the waitress asked us for our order, and without hesitation, he ordered us each a shot of Rakia, which is a brandy and the national drink in Bulgaria. I hated the stuff but was forced to partake. While in Bulgaria, I once had a terrible sore throat, and a lady friend that I was with poured the brandy on a white T-shirt that she pulled out of my closet, and applied fresh ground black pepper to it. She applied it on my throat, and within hours, the relief began to kick in, as well as my energy.

Once the drink order was placed, considering the strong likelihood of someone listening in, I responded to his concern about the visa. "Dimitri," I said, "we can obviously make a case for you and will get back to you at the appropriate time." I left the issue of the visa on the table in hopes for him to see a viable exchange was, in fact, possible. He was appreciative, and before I could say another word, he looked at me and asked what the need for all the security was? With a slight smirk and laugh, he followed up by saying, "Look, I know all these guys, so don't bother." I politely explained that it was embassy protocol to have them and that I had no option but to take the resources. At that moment, the waitress returned with more Rakia and Dimitri grabbed his first order and in one motion, made it disappear. I, having no choice, followed his lead, and before I was able to gasp for air, a new drink was waiting for me. I was going to be in trouble. As a non-drinker, this was going to finish horribly and not in my favor.

He then leaned forward and explained how he has property in Virginia and was recently denied a visa from the American Embassy. He explained that he needed to return to the United States to take care of his personal affairs. He asked again for my assistance. I sympathized with him and acknowledged the sense of urgency, but I also capitalized by raising the need to resolve the issue of fugitive Peter Simenov. I told him, if this was resolved, then and only then could we entertain his request. To my complete surprise, he responded by saying, "Don't worry about Peter. He will do what I tell him to do."

Like that, it seemed to be done! It was at that moment when I heard in his voice his willingness to cooperate and without warning, I had the urge to grab my drink and cheer in Bulgarian. "*Nazdráve!*" Everyone in close proximity stopped talking and looked over to see what had happened. They immediately realized who was in my presence and promptly returned to their business. His security folks were a bit startled as well, and once they realized their boss was fine, removed their hands from their jackets. Dimitri seemed startled by my outburst and not only joined in and laughed with me but took the opportunity to toast to the idea of having an exchange take place with the "Americans" so that everyone looked good. He obviously wanted to help Boyko get in good with the Americans, he wanted his visa to enter the United States, and Peter was on his own. As far as Dimitri was concerned, this was a business deal that made complete sense. Peter, due to his own carelessness in New York, now brought attention to Dimitri, unwanted attention at that, and he needed to get his boss out of it.

Sometime later, I received an interesting phone call from a Bulgarian woman who worked tirelessly in getting her country to move in the right direction. She called me in October 2004, approximately 1 year after I left Bulgaria, and she was in shock. She said, "The news here has just reported that Dimitri was gunned down in front of his bodyguards in downtown Sofia." I immediately felt a chill go up my spine as the news was relayed to me.

These people were basically one step above "primitive," and they were hungry to both protect their interests, and above all, did not worry about being investigated. The police worked for them, and the prosecutors did as they were told, so no one in government was a threat. The only issue for them at this time is a quasi-political request by the Secret Service and one special agent—me—who was pushing the official request to have Simenov surrender and on his own so as to fly back with me to the United States.

My road to Bulgaria was not planned or one which I would have fore-seen by any means. Outside of the gun permit I received to allow me to carry during my time in country, a paycheck, and a "safe house" to use, when my cases require it, nothing more was done to secure, fund, or establish a comprehensive plan to secure my safety, or more importantly, to execute our mission in the country. We were an agen-cy tasked with a dual mission, but when it came to investigations at that time, we simply just lacked "depth." Once again, I had reached a level of frustration with my agency's lack of expertise and endurance to conduct sophisticated, long-term, financial fraud investigations.

This void resurfaced and continued to chip away at me, and I had enough of it. The overseas assignments were filled around the protec-tion assignments, despite the fact that there was a great deal of good work to do, but no one to do it. So, while sitting at my desk in the Rome Field Office, I submitted my letter of resignation with the intent to work in another government agency. No sooner did I submit my letter, a disagreement occurred between a trusted colleague and my-self, which resulted in me losing a friendship and my assignment in Rome. The disagreement also impacted my decision to return to the United States and work for another agency. The final outcome since the agent replacing me was already notified, was for me to return to Secret Service headquarters, Washington, D.C., go to Sofia, Bulgaria, or Istanbul, Turkey.

I chose Bulgaria because I knew that the women were beautiful and that the assignment was going to be risky, and I was ready for both. Mentally, I immediately adjusted and focused on the new assignment. My personal belongings, including my immaculate 1984, completely restored, red, 911 Porsche Carrera and my brand-new motorcycle, a BMW K-1200RS, were put in storage, and my apartment in the exclusive neighborhood of Parioli, located on Via Achiemede, near Piazza Euclide, Rome, was returned to the embassy. With a one-way ticket, off to Sofia, Bulgaria, I went. What was replacing my beautiful apartment in Rome was a furnished apartment that agents rotating out of Sofia working counterfeit cases used to debrief informants; thus, a whole bunch of unknowns.

In any event, the new journey began in May of 2002. I was on a 2-hour Alitalia flight from Rome to Sofia. It had just landed at Sofia airport, and we began to taxi to the gate. I recall what I call my last contact with an Italian woman on that particular flight. I was sitting in the very front of the plane, always in an aisle seat, a strategic place for armed agents. There, I was making direct eye contact, followed by an occasional flirtatious smile, toward the beautiful flight attendant.

She was a tall, northern Italian blonde with an athletic build who seemed opened to exchanging eye contact. The last glance quickly turned into a quick exchange of words. I conditioned myself to initiate all of my conversations with Italian women in English. This was simply done to ensure that they understood I was a foreigner. Through my prior personal experiences, this approach would prove to be the "answer" to my dating experiences in Italy. I immediately secured an invite for dinner in Rome and her cell number. I was obviously not thinking this is an Italian woman, and she was going to look for a tentative schedule prior to embarking. In my mind, I was simply hoping that she believed I was on a business trip to Bulgaria and would return. Look, I had great plans already in mind. I was going to wine and dine this 5 foot 7 babe at my favorite part of Rome, Testachicco. Hey, it would be just a matter of time the Rome office would ask me to help out on a protective assignment, so why not just keep things under wraps.

But just before grabbing my bags, she had an opportunity to ask where I lived and if I was returning home tomorrow since she was going to be off for a few days and should we get together? I had no choice responding in Italian, but as if I were a foreigner speaking. I told her I was going to be living somewhere in Sofia and no longer Rome. With a puzzled, almost angry look on her face, she carefully glanced around to ensure no one was listening, and without hesitation, responded in Italian, "Are you serious? You are going to live in that dumpy place? Don't bother calling me!" Trust me, her response, spoken in Italian, was unbelievably sexy to hear! Upon parking at the gate, I got up with a look of disgust, grabbed my bag, and with no motivation to pretend to be a resident of Rome, responded back by saying, "Yes, well, I live here now. I guess you're right—dinner is off."

As I cleared customs and grabbed my bags, I stepped out and was struck by the cold gray air of Bulgaria. I immediately entered the dark SUV awaiting me and was greeted by a colleague I will only identify and Michael and an embassy driver. I didn't speak a word of the Slavic language . . . This was going to be interesting.

As I explained in Chapter One, Sofia, Bulgaria, was not a pretty place. I had visited it prior for a few days when I was assigned to the Rome office. I was there to assist another colleague who was working counterfeit cases with the National Police Service, the Bulgarian police. Sofia was a gray city, cold, and in many ways, it seemed like a place still stuck in the early Soviet era of the 1970s. What made it worse were the inadequate training, equipment, and most of all, substandard salaries paid to police officers. The average monthly salary of a Bulgarian police officer varied from 500 lev for a new police officer to 900 lev for those with extensive professional experience. The average monthly salary in Bulgaria is some 600 lev, which is approximately $300.00 in the United States and this gives you a great comparison to how little the police in Bulgaria are paid to others around the world.

It reminded me like nothing back home, and more importantly, I didn't speak the language, so for me, very little was attractive other than my job assignment. I was fortunate that many Bulgarians did speak English, and the informants who I dealt with spoke English. In other instances, I relied on a select few from the U.S. Embassy to engage my Bulgarian counterparts, but for the most part, I had to rely on my instincts and street experience to decipher who was being more truthful and whether I was being set up.

The National Police Service is responsible for combating general crime and supporting the operations of other law enforcement agencies in Bulgaria, like the National Investigative Service and the Central Office for Combating Organized Crime. The Police Service has criminal and financial sections across both national and local offices. They were the ones that investigated counterfeit cases. Now, prior to Bulgaria, I had limited exposure to counterfeit currency investigations. In Rome, we would receive an occasional request for support from the United States, but for the most part, it was running a suspected note through our counterfeit database, and then shipping it to our headquarters for further analysis or just logged as evidence.

When at the New York Field Office, one of the most active offices investigating counterfeit currency due to the Gotti case, I spent no time working counterfeit currency investigations. Nonetheless, it didn't matter. Counterfeit cases were worked similarly to how one would work a low-level drug case. The goal in most scenarios was to purchase through the use of an undercover operative or an informant a series of samples, thus hoping to work up the "food chain" until you have a main distributor or a possible stash house.

Now, with counterfeit currency, the goal is suppress the note that is being counterfeited, and most of our bosses believed that by getting to the "counterfeit plant," which was the location where the counterfeit currency was produced, meant basically the end of the investigation. Well, let me say that this approach might have been true in the "old days" where the use of printing presses were facilitated in the production of the currency, but with the age of computers and high-tech printers, mobility became an issue and the "art" in fabricating the counterfeit plates was removed.

Thus, the folks engaging in such activities had minimal experience and were able to produce a relatively high-quality product in short order. The crooks immediately abandoned the old method, a means that required creating a negative plate of a certain denomination, then producing the actual engraved plate which allowed the mass production of a particular denomination/currency, and finding a printing press similar to the ones used to crank out newspapers to fabricate the counterfeit. Yet, once the new method computers and laser printers came into play, it replaced the old means and the Service was on a completely different playing field when it came to locating and dismounting an operation. With smaller-sized equipment, a plant was mobile and easily transferable and became very difficult to locate.

Chapter One briefly described my time in Bulgaria and how the main focus of that assignment was to locate and return to justice a fugitive by the name of Peter Simenov. "Petar" as he was called in Bulgaria. He was a Bulgarian citizen, and in Bulgaria, the extradition of its citizens was not permissible and if so, extremely problematic due to the limited agreement in place between the U.S. and Bulgaria concerning such matters. Simenov, upon making bail, grabbed the first flight to Bulgaria and was never seen again.

Anyway, I knew nothing about the case until the Counterfeit Division at headquarters got ahold of me and asked me to look into finding the fugitive. My boss, Ralph, the special agent in charge of the Rome Field Office, felt that locating and bringing Peter Simenov to the U.S. was going to make me a "star" in the Secret Service. He knew how much I enjoyed investigations and the difficulty I had with wearing both a protection and investigative hat when both required extensive attention to detail. In his mind, this assignment would keep me focused for at least 6 months doing just criminal work. I was slightly confused, me being a star. Heck, I thought the Secret Service had that one well covered.

OK, why not? Let's go get this fuckin' fugitive. So I immediately went to work. The first thing was to share the warrant and all details available about him with both Europol and Interpol. Europol was fairly a new organization then, but I did everything that I could in notifying the appropriate authorities in order to make Simenov's travels within Europe, as well as elsewhere, very difficult. I did not assume that Simenov was traveling under his real name. Obtaining a passport in a different name and new identity was not a difficult task in Bulgaria.

I began to develop an investigative plan comprised of trusted sources. In addition to the sources, the RSO's shop and an agency I will not mention provided assets that helped locate the fugitive. In no time at all, I began to get information that this Simenov was in Sofia, and that he was reporting to a Russian who ran one of the most powerful organized crime syndicates in Bulgaria. Peter's boss was Dimitri Minev aka "the Russian," and Meniv was on everyone's investigative radar except the Bulgarian police radar. I was fortunate to have the hard-charging U.S. Ambassador James W. Pardew in country. The ambassador greatly supported U.S. law enforcement activities in Bulgaria, and with his support and that of my boss in Rome, I had every intention to contribute to the cause.

After our brief encounter in the nightclub, I met Peter at noon that very next day at the Borisova Gradina Park. I was standing next to the statue of Bratska Mogila as I had informed Peter I would be, but I was not alone. It was cold, and I had added a few more layers of clothing to my standard attire: fitted black fleece gloves and a black ski hat. The surveillance team from the embassy was in place. Roberto was there with his team, and it wasn't long after 12 noon that I noticed from a distance the figure of the man I was waiting for. Peter. He saw me and without delay, joked about the location and time of the meeting. He had obviously had a rough night and was still in his nightclub attire. Regardless of his condition, I got straight to the point. I identified myself, showed him my Secret Service credentials, and explained to him that it would be in his best interest to cooperate and return back to the United States. He smirked and arrogantly responded by telling me he was Bulgarian and there was no extradition treaty, so I should go fuck myself. I paused and took in a deep breath and upon exhaling, I explained to him that I was not going back to the U.S. without him and that when I did, I was not going alone. Again, he laughed.

Peter was conflicted. While he felt safe and secure in Bulgaria, at the same time, he also felt trapped. I needed to keep him trapped until I found a solution to the issue. I was determined to hold to my promise and only leave Bulgaria with him in tow. So for the next several months, I worked on various options in an effort to catch a break. At first, I was hopefully optimistic. The possibility of a rendition looked promising, but after several "high-level" meetings, including one with the prime minister, things began to take a turn—and not in my favor but rather Peter's. We were able to coordinate a meeting with the prime minister. The bosses came in from Rome, and we broke the ice by complimenting the prime minister for his ability to speak Italian. It seemed to work, but after several flattering statements, he turned, and with a motionless face and in Italian so none of the Bulgarians could hear, explained that, unfortunately, there was no political will to grant such an operation. I needed to find an alternative route.

The very next week as I sat down for a one-on-one with the Deputy Minister of Interior Boyko Borrisov, during our routine update meetings where we discussed various counterfeiting cases, I brought up the name Peter Simenov. I explained the case and how important this fugitive's return to the U.S. would be to our relationship. Boyko was not stupid. He saw this as an opportunity to bridge a stronger relationship with the United States. This was a negotiation in which he held some major cards. He needed an alliance outside of the "old," long-established relationship with mother Russia, which he was looking to balance with new ties to Washington. He quickly recommended an operation which would solve this matter. I responded by highlighting the risks associated with such an operation.

Within minutes, he was on the phone with his old cronies at SIC. Boyko was once a part of SIC. Now a wealthy man, he had turned a new leaf and focused on doing good deeds for Bulgaria. As explained, SIC was an insurance company run by the Bulgarian Mafia, and one of the founders, who was on the phone with Boyko, was Dimitri Minev. Peter reported to Minev, and Boyko was speaking to him in front of me on the ministry hard line. What the fuck! When he got off the phone, he said, "You have a meeting with Meniv." Meniv was aware of the situation and is willing to meet to discuss particulars.

Through the translator, I was told where to meet Meniv. With that said, I had just enough time to brief the bosses, as well as prepare for the meeting. The bosses in Rome were excited, and headquarters started to get very interested, and I was briefing them more and more each day. I was not worried, and I guess in some ways not concerned for whatever reason, but I was definitely now in the crosshairs. Someone or something had to give, but when and exactly where I had no clue. I mean, let's be honest . . . How many situations like this can we honestly say go without a hitch? Not many are what I now realize, but I must say, I was on a high for such a long time, it didn't really matter to me. I may have incorrectly believed that good would overcome evil all the time, and since I was doing the right thing, I therefore had nothing to worry about.

As my assignment was coming to an end, I grew increasingly disillusioned with the Bulgarians. One day, I received a call from my boss in Rome. He was very vague and in an almost dry tone, explained how the FBI had received a call from the German police, the Bundeskriminalamt "BKA." They thought that the agent in Bulgaria was from the FBI so they initially contacted them. After some research, the FBI called the Secret Service in Washington, and it was cleared up. The Germans wanted to speak to us. So the BKA had some information on "our" informants in Bulgaria, and I was instructed to, when possible, coordinate my travels to meet with them.

I contacted the Secret Service agent assigned at Interpol who was coordinating the meeting. So I flew to Germany and headed straight to the city of Wiesbaden where the headquarters for the BKA was located. The folks there were all very quiet and with a look of surprise, asked me if I was the agent living in Bulgaria. I respond yes, as I proudly displayed my Secret Service credentials and diplomatic passport. The meeting started with them handing me transcripts of an intercepted conversation between a Bulgarian Mafia figure they were targeting and an unknown Bulgarian living in Sofia. The conversation evolved around growing frustration that was brewing with certain factions of the Mafia in Bulgaria. Whatever the issue, the order was passed, and it was very clear: ***Kill the informant and if you can, kill the agent as well***.

My mouth dropped, I had really nothing to say. I was alone, and now, armed with this information, I was in deep trouble. Upon my return to Sofia, I immediately stopped all communication with the informants and halted all meetings with the Bulgarian authorities with the exception of Boyko. I immediately spoke with Boyko and told him of the threat, minus who gave me the information. I was furious, to say the least, and so was he. I was only in country for, at most, 2 weeks, but reflecting back, it was an unwise decision, and we the Secret Service were just not prepared for it.

Boyko was crushed upon hearing the news. We had gotten along well, and he was frustrated. He knew this was not a good thing, in particular as it related to his relationship with the U.S. ambassador and his desire to forge a strong partnership with the U.S. I briefed other assets that week, and on Sunday morning, while having breakfast at the Hilton Restaurant with others from the embassy, I was interrupted from eating by two hulking men. They asked me to accompany them to the Ministry of Interior for a very sensitive meeting. I was wearing my Adidas workout gear and sneakers. Unshaven and wearing a baseball cap, I asked if I could go to my apartment to get properly dressed. With no hesitation, the two gorillas said no. So I looked at my friends and wondered what this was but placed trust in the men to being who they said they were. Rob knew what to do. He immediately called the local assets, and before I got off the hotel elevator and in the car with them, it was confirmed that this was a legitimate meeting. A text message from one of the folks in a certain agency gave me assurances that this was legitimate.

Boyko was at one end of his table, a long one that could seat all his generals, if need be. On one side of that table, Boyko's left, sat, in order, a general, a colonel, and a major, all known to me and to the Secret Service. On the other side of the table, Boyko's left, was I. Standing behind the general was the translator. She began to translate, and it was not good news. Boyko was angry. At one point, he was actually screaming at the top of his lungs, upset by the latest news he heard of his guest (me) being threatened. As I was sitting there, I hoped that nothing had happened to my informants and realized that from this point forward, until I leave this country, I now have an even bigger bull's-eye on my back. As far as the informants, these 9 months spending countless hours with both, I began to grow close to them and saw them a bit differently, which, of course, could be dangerous.

Anyway, I recall looking down at the table in front of me, sort of the same way my son now would do when being reprimanded. I was so embarrassed for them and of what I was hearing, I just couldn't look at them. That is, until the one in the middle, the colonel, began to cry. He was, in my opinion, the least corrupt and who genuinely wanted me to date his daughter and possibly take her away from Bulgaria and give her a better life. He had lived a life filled with corruption, deception, and death, and may have wanted his daughter to not be exposed to it. My courage returned, and as the words spewed out of Boyko's mouth, I looked up at each and every one of those men straight in their eyes, and after it was all over, they were told to submit their resignations. On those words, they stood at attention and saluted Boyko. The colonel looked at me, and with tears in his eyes, said in broken English, "Sorry, Nino, sorry, Nino." I just looked and within seconds, they had emptied the room.

My time in Bulgaria was over, and as I boarded my flight back to U.S., with a quick connection in Frankfurt, Germany, I was handed a gift from Deputy Minister of Interior Boyko Borrisov, who accompanied me to the runway in his personal armored vehicle. The gift was an exact replica sword of the one worn by King Ferdinand I of Bulgaria. I was shocked, and as he walked off the plane, his motorcade waiting and men dressed in ceremonial uniforms, saluting, he turned with one last wave and departed the runway.

About The Author

Nino Perrotta is a highly accomplished law enforcement professional with more than 20 years of experience in military, security, and protective services, with expertise in threat analysis/mitigation, physical and facility security, major event logistics, and VIP travel. Nino has successfully conducted complex investigations, both domestically and abroad. He has a proven track record and ability to liaise with diverse stakeholders across agencies and countries.

In 1990, after receiving his Army Commission from Fordham University, Nino embarked on his military training at Fort Huachuca, Arizona. There, he completed both the officer basic military intelligence training and advance counterintelligence training, resulting in his appointment as a counterintelligence officer, United States Army Reserves.

In 1993, he began his career in law enforcement as one of the first "all-civilian" investigators for Mayor David Dinkins's newly created New York City Civilian Complaint Review Board (CCRB). The CCRB's mission was to investigate, mediate, make findings, and recommend courses of action on complaints against New York City Police Officers. These complaints often alleged the use of excessive or unnecessary force, abuse of authority, discourtesy, or the use of offensive language toward the public.

In 1994, after completing the Rockland County Police Academy, Nino was assigned to the Bronx County District Attorney's Detective Investigators Bureau. During his tenure at the DA's office, Nino expanded his investigative experience while assigned to a low-level gambling investigation, the focus of which was gambling and loan-sharking activities of Gambino crime family "soldier" Greg DePalma. Through his leadership, tenacity, and superior investigative skills, the investigation blossomed. Prior to Nino's departure to the United States Secret Service in 1995, the investigation was ready to target the head of the Gambino crime family, John A. Gotti Junior.

After a tour at the Secret Service's New York Field Office, where Nino conducted numerous other financial and electronic crimes investigations, he was assigned to the Field Office in Rome, Italy.

While overseas, Nino conducted numerous protective security advances for both the president and former presidents of the United States. Nino also worked closely with the Italian authorities on fraud, financial, and cybercrime investigations with global implications.

Nino collaborated with the Italian Finance Police (Guardia di Finanza) on one such investigation which identified a scheme in Pescara, Italy. The perpetrators, Italian university professors, were defrauding the city of Pescara with a sophisticated prime bank lending scheme posing as members of the U.S. Federal Reserve Bank who claimed unrealistic return on government investments.

Nino was then assigned to Bucharest, Romania, to address the growth of computer hacking and fraud cases against U.S. companies and government agencies.

In Romania, Nino continued his track record of conducting

high-impact successful investigations which led to the prosecution of numerous Romanian criminals. Nino leveraged this success, along with his strong interpersonal skills, toward the establishment of a mutually cooperative and beneficial relationship between Romania and the Secret Service. These cooperative efforts with the Romanian authorities helped justify the funding and establishment of a permanent Secret Service presence in country.

Following his successful tenure in Romania, Nino was then sent to Sophia, Bulgaria, for a 9-month assignment, the purpose of which was to replicate his efforts in Romania; namely, the establishment of a Secret Service office in Bulgaria. He quickly went to work establishing liaisons and partnerships with both Bulgarian law and nonlaw enforcement, as well as with the private sector. During his time in Bulgaria, Nino placed great emphasis on collaboration, information sharing, and strategic partnerships.

Nino also coordinated investigative action and initiatives aimed at combatting the counterfeiting of U.S. currency. One case involved the tracking, location, and apprehension by Nino of a fugitive who returned to Bulgaria after being indicted by the Secret Service in New York for counterfeit currency violations.

Nino obtained the trust and confidence of senior-ranking officials in the Bulgarian Ministry of Interior. In 2002, along with the support of the American embassy, he was able to establish, in Bulgaria, the first "International" Secret Service Electronic Crimes Task Force (ECTF). Nino utilized, as a model, the extremely successful New York ECTF. He was fortunate to have been part of this ECTF.

In 2003, upon the conclusion of his foreign tour of duty, Nino was assigned to the Secret Service Intelligence Division in Washington,

D.C., at which time he represented the Service at the newly created U.S. Department of Homeland Security National Operations Center (NOC).

At the NOC, Nino helped deliver real-time situational awareness and monitored homeland defense and security issues. He successfully worked with governors, homeland security advisors, law enforcement partners, and critical infrastructure operators in all 50 states and 50+ major urban areas nationwide. Nino went on to become the assistant senior watch officer, office of the under secretary, responsible for the coordination, collection, and fusion of information from more than 35 federal, state, territorial, tribal, local, and private sector agencies.

Since 2004, Nino has been a senior special agent with a United States government agency and plans to retire August 2017.

In addition to an accomplished professional career, Nino holds a BA and MA in political science from Fordham University, New York, New York. He is also a graduate of both the Federal Law Enforcement Training Center, Glynco, Georgia, and the United States Secret Service Academy, Laurel, Maryland.

Some noteworthy awards bestowed upon Nino include:
- Special award for prosecution of Seynabou Seck in the Southern District of New York and the Prime Bank Lending Scheme in Pescara, Italy.
- New York State Law Enforcement Award for investigation and prosecution of John A. Gotti and the Gambino crime family.
- FBI award for investigation into European-American bank robberies.

Nino is an accomplished hunter who loves the outdoors, and in 2012, sold a successful start-up construction company based in Washington, D.C., that he founded in 2004. Today, he is the proud owner of Sequoia Security Group Inc., based in Washington, D.C.

CPSIA information can be obtained
at www.ICGtesting.com
Printed in the USA
BVHW022247010421
603811BV00004B/92